D1435539

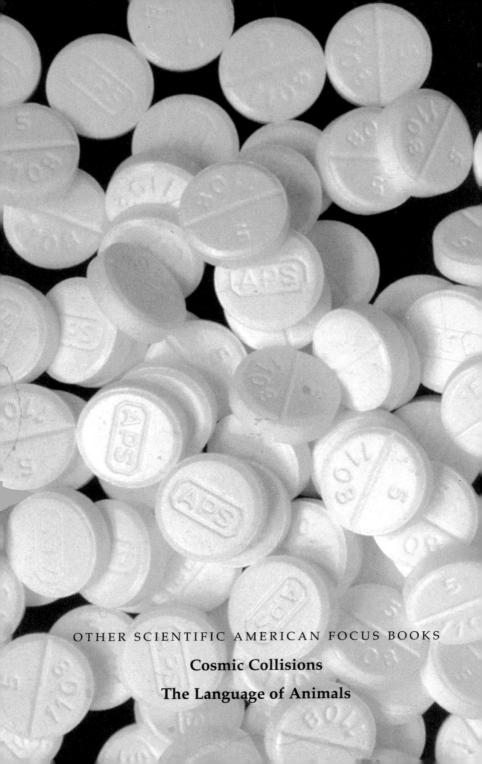

MEDICATION
OF THE
MIND

SCOTT VEGGEBERG

Foreword by Richard Restak, M.D.

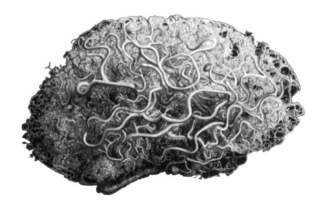

A SCIENTIFIC AMERICAN FOCUS BOOK

Henry Holt and Company
New York

Henry Holt and Company, Inc.
Publishers since 1866
115 West 18th Street
New York, New York 10011

Henry Holt ® is a registered trademark
of Henry Holt and Company, Inc.

Published in Canada by Fitzhenry & Whiteside Ltd.,
195 Allstate Parkway, Markham, Ontario L3R 4T8.

Library of Congress Cataloging-in-Publication Data
Veggeberg, Scott.
Medication of the Mind / by Scott Veggeberg;
foreword by Richard Restak.
p.   cm.—(A Scientific American Focus book)
Includes index.
1. Psychiatry—Philosophy. 2. Mental illness—Chemotherapy.
3. Mental illness—Treatment. 4. Biological psychiatry
I. Title. II. Series.
RC437.5.V44 1996   95-34584
616.89'18—dc20   CIP

ISBN 0-8050-3841-8
ISBN 0-8050-3842-6 (An Owl Book: pbk.)

Henry Holt books are available for special promotions
and premiums. For details contact: Director, Special Markets.

First Edition—1996

Conceived by Robert Ubell Associates, Inc.
Project Director: Robert N. Ubell
Project Manager: Luis A. Gonzalez
Art Direction: J.C. Suarès
Design: Amy Gonzalez
Production: Christy Trotter

Printed in the United States of America

All first editions are printed on acid-free paper.∞

10 9 8 7 6 5 4 3 2 1
10 9 8 7 6 5 4 3 2 1 (pbk.)

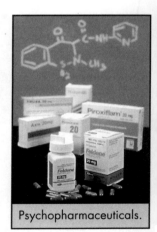

Psychopharmaceuticals.

C O N T E N T S

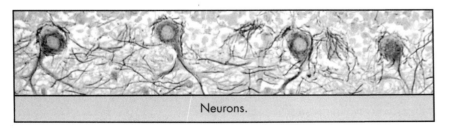

Neurons.

Richard Restak, M.D., George Washington University

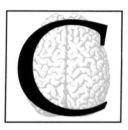hemicals capable of influencing the brain and behavior have been employed for thousands of years. Ancient Indian texts describe the prescription of the plant *Rauwolfia serpentina* to calm agitated and overwrought patients. Research in the 1950s revealed the plant's active ingredient to be reserpine, which went on to become the first commonly employed antipsychotic. Other mind-altering natural chemicals chemically identified at about the same time include peyote, mescaline and other "magic intoxicants" gathered in the jungles of South America and throughout the western part of the Amazon basin. Albert Hofmann's synthesis of LSD provided yet another clue that, in his words, "certain mental illness that were supposed to be of purely psychic nature had a biochemical cause." The search over the past three decades for these biochemical influences in health and disease has spurred a revolutionary change in our ideas about the nature of our thoughts, emotions and behavior. Psychological theories have yielded place to an emphasis on neurochemistry and research aimed at synthesizing new and more powerful psychotropic drugs.

Early advances depended very much on happenstance and just plain luck. Thorazine, the antipsychotic responsible for the discharge of emotionally ill patients from mental hospitals into the community of thousands, serendipitously resulted from research aimed at developing a new antihistamine for use in surgery. The monoamine oxidase inhibitors, antidepressants still in use today, emerged from a chance observation of the mood-elevating effects of a drug used in the treatment of tuberculosis. Lithium, a natural element now employed to equilibrate moods in manic depressives, evolved from the arbitrary selection and administration in an experiment of the most soluble form of uric acid, lithium urate.

This "hit-and-miss" approach to chemical brain research would have continued were it not for the development of one unifying and liberating conceptual breakthrough—the discovery of receptors. The fit of a neurotransmitter, one of the brain's chemical messengers, to its receptor is often compared to that of a key to its lock. While helpful, the analogy is somewhat oversimplified since receptors are not solid and unchanging like locks and keys, but proteins located within the membrane of the living, ever-changing nerve cell. Like all proteins within living organisms, receptors can undergo changes in structure and shape, and in some cases can even change their identity so as to accept new or structurally similar neurotransmitters. The first generation of psychotropic drugs developed on the basis of receptor research were "dirty" drugs—they affected more than one neurotransmitter-receptor pair. As a result, such drugs had many side effects, some so distressing to the patients that they would rather continue to suffer from their illness. But with additional research, neuropharmacologists honed their knowledge and skills enough to synthesize a new generation of "clean" drugs aimed at affecting a single receptor. Prozac, Zoloft and Paxil are the first products resulting from efforts to develop receptor-specific drugs. The effectiveness in the treatment of depression of these serotonin-reuptake blockers (so named because of their ability to enhance the amount of available serotonin in the synaptic gap between nerve cells) has exceeded the expectations of even the most demanding patients and doctors alike. But perhaps their most intriguing success has come from the positive effects of these drugs on people affected by mild impairments, people who have continued to function despite their depressions and, in many cases, who don't strike others as being impaired. What does it say about the human mind when one's general feeling of the world and one's place in it can be modified by a chemical that, in many instances, acts so subtly that the person taking the drug experiences few or no side effects or other experiences usually associated with the taking of a medication? While ethicists and others ponder such questions, the development of the next generation of mind-brain-altering chemicals continues to unfold.

Already, medications aimed at the enhancement of memory seem feasible based on research aimed at developing drugs for Alzheimer's disease—demonstrating that efforts aimed at relieving the plight of unfortunate members of society can sometimes rebound to the benefit of the healthy. But we must never forget that we are symbol- and language-driven creatures whose humanity can never be completely accounted for by chemistry. We are influenced by words, concepts and fantasies—as Freud and others have correctly maintained. But this does not imply an either/or approach towards correcting disturbances in our thoughts and feelings—either "talk" therapy or neurotransmitter approaches. The words and concepts that stir us do so by altering the chemical make-up of our brain, and in this process there is time and place aplenty for the humanistic influences that distinguish us from all other creatures. Our mind and brain are like two sides of one coin: if we look at the coin from one side, it appears to be all biology; turn the coin over, and we encounter the subjective world of thoughts and dreams and images that comprise the human mind. To that extent we are hybrid creatures—not entirely servants of biology, yet not entirely independent of the influences imposed upon us by the structure and function of our brain. Various forms of psychotherapy, defined here as approaches to emotional disorders that don't involve drugs and don't necessarily require reference to the brain, will continue to be valid. Emotional illness always occurs in a context; often the skillful manipulation of that context, and the sufferer's response to it, can offer more benefit than any chemical presently available, or ever likely to be devised.

Can Prozac Replace
Freud?

The brain remains the most mysterious organ in our bodies. We know there are about 100 billion neurons in the brain, but neuroscientists still do not have a clear idea of why, for instance, six million of our brain cells must be called into action just to tell the difference between the sweet odor of bananas and the pungent smell of beer.

But the brain is hardly the black box of unknown function that has defied explanation for thousands of years. Today, scientists know a great deal about how the brain works at the cellular and biochemical levels. In fact, many neuroscientists now believe that the way we think is primarily determined by our brain chemistry and by the complex interactions of the trillions of connections between neurons called synapses.

Many believe that all our thoughts, dreams and emotions—everything that constitutes the ethereal substance we call the mind—is a result of the intricate interplay of chemistry and connections. It's only recently that we have discovered that different brain functions are located in different areas and that the brain works by a process known as "distributed parallel processing" and not as a whole organ working all at once. As you read these words, specific portions of the back of the brain associated with reading are active, along with other areas along the side that deal with words and still others in the frontal lobes of the brain that put the picture together. With brain imaging techniques such as PET and MRI scans, you can actually watch these areas "light up" with activity.

Mental illness is now thought to be a disruption of the orderly processing of complex information. It's as if the brain were composed of many separate computers, all working on different problems or aspects of the same problem, all tied together in a network. If one computer goes down, or if the network fails to pass along information properly, the system crashes; the mind becomes unbalanced. The brain, however, is not a microprocessor, and the

Prozac
capsules.

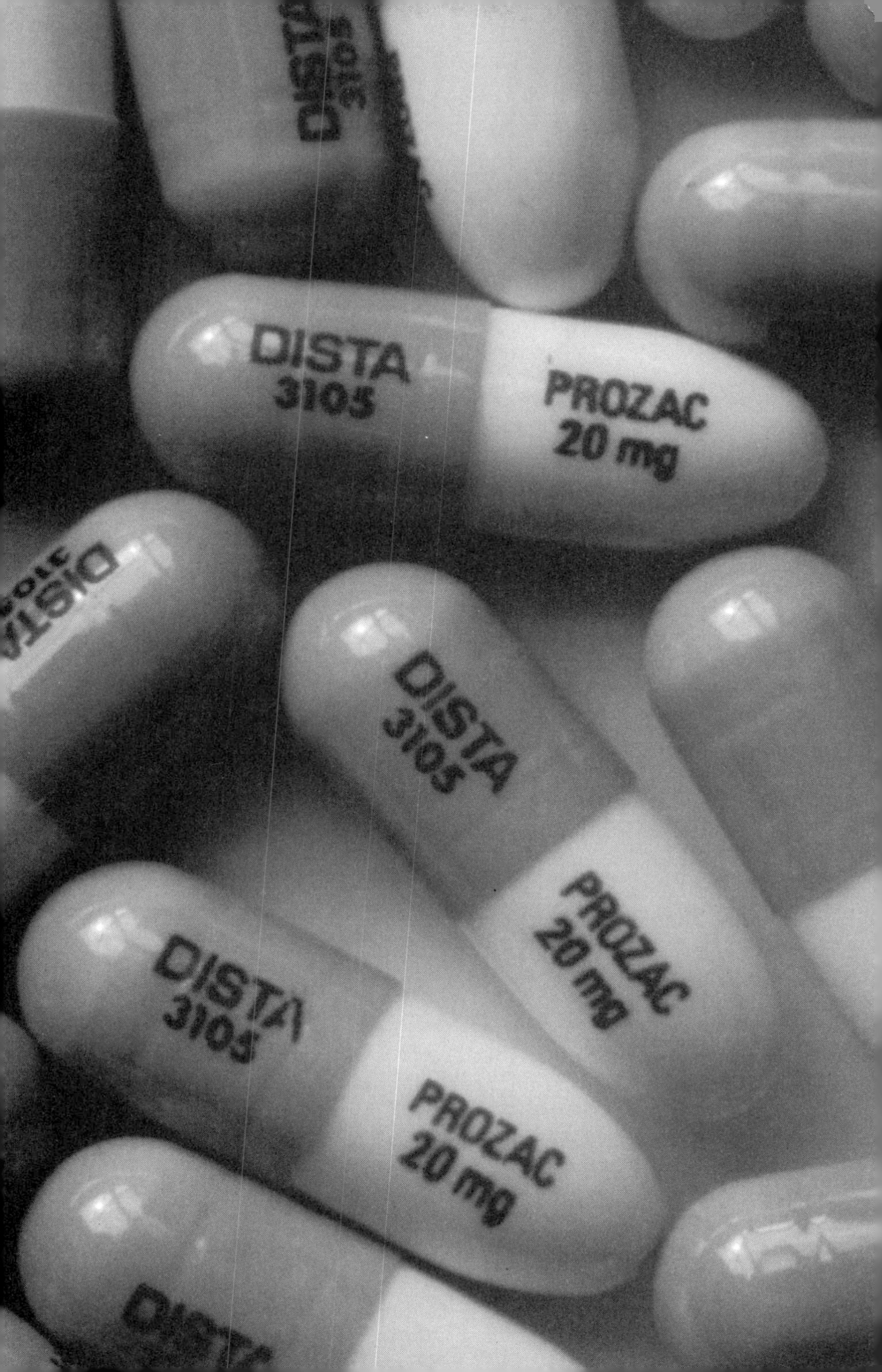
DISTA
3105
PROZAC
20 mg

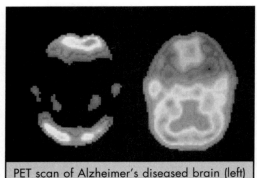

PET scan of Alzheimer's diseased brain (left) and normal one (right).

mind is not a computer program. The brain is an organ that runs on biochemistry, not electricity. From this perspective, the best way to help an ailing mind is to treat the brain like any other organ, providing it with drugs to attempt to restore its biochemical balance.

This is the basis of what has been called the "biological revolution" in psychiatry. The current trend among neuroscientists and psychiatrists is to view mental illness as an organic disease that is caused by defective brain function rather than by swirling streams of subconscious thought manifesting themselves as physical and mental symptoms. Although as we will see, upbringing, society, childhood traumas and everything that falls into the definition of environment are still thought to be important factors in shaping how our minds are shaped. For instance, only about one percent of the population is afflicted with schizophrenia. However, when one identical twin is diagnosed with schizophrenia, the other twin has about a 50 percent chance of developing the same disease. What this tells us is that genes are quite important in this mental illness, but some sort of as-yet-unexplained environmental factors must also be playing a large role.

Still, the view of mental illness as an organic disease is predominant, and today there are drugs like chlorpromazine for schizophrenia and lithium for bipolar disorder, as we will see in chapter 3. There are new mind medicines—Prozac and Zoloft, to name just two—that lift the dark clouds of depression. Indeed, it's claimed that these new antidepressants can even go further. According to Peter Kramer, author of the controversial *Listening to Prozac*, antidepressant drugs not only make sick minds well, but in many cases can make well minds better, imparting a brighter, more positive attitude than ever before.

Some psychiatrists maintain their faith in the talk therapy pioneered by Sigmund Freud—whose work will be explored in chapter 8—and their belief that mental illness is not an organic disease. They contend that childhood traumas or other environmental factors play the biggest role in mental disease. Advocates of the psychotherapeutic approach to treating major mental illness, such as Peter Breggin, author of *Toxic Psychiatry* and *Talking Back to Prozac*, argue that we are not ruled simply by our inborn brain chemistry. Breggin contends that our nurture–our upbringing and environment–plays the most critical role in shaping our minds. This argument will be detailed in chapter 9. But, for today at least, the thinking is that nature, not nurture, holds the greatest sway in determining how we think and act. And drug therapy seems to offer the

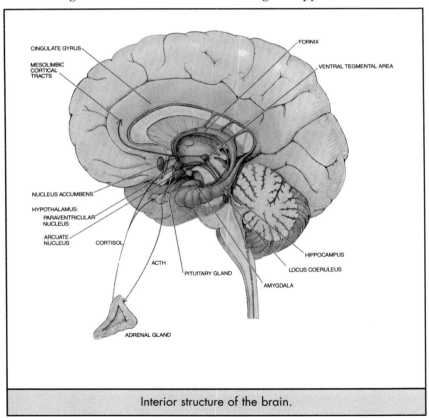

CINGULATE GYRUS

MESOLIMBIC CORTICAL TRACTS

FORNIX

VENTRAL TEGMENTAL AREA

NUCLEUS ACCUMBENS

HYPOTHALAMUS:
PARAVENTRICULAR NUCLEUS

ARCUATE NUCLEUS

CORTISOL

ACTH

PITUITARY GLAND

AMYGDALA

HIPPOCAMPUS

LOCUS COERULEUS

ADRENAL GLAND

Interior structure of the brain.

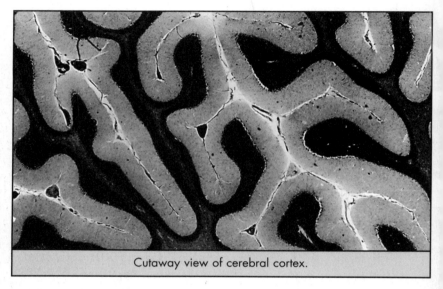
Cutaway view of cerebral cortex.

best hope of altering the course of serious mental illness.

If it is indeed nature that rules the mind, then it is our genes that determine that nature. A disturbing question that we are just beginning to ask is: can we control this genetic predisposition through drugs, and through genetic engineering? Can violence, obesity and racism be bred out of us? And is this something we even want to do?

For now, though, we will explore the neurons, the place where psychopharmaceuticals do their work to soothe a troubled mind, followed by a look at how specific mind medicines work. Chapters 4 and 5 will provide more background on how the brain is put together and how this collection of 100 billion neurons coalesces to form the mind. Chapter 6 examines what is known about the causes and symptoms of the major mental illnesses, followed by a brief look at psychotherapy in chapter 7. We'll wrap up our tour of the world of mind medicines in chapters 8 and 9 with a discussion of how our view of the mind has evolved over the past few thousand years from a belief that madness was caused by evil demons to today's view of the mind as simply the sum total of the workings of the neurochemical organ called the brain.

Cutaway view of a neuron.

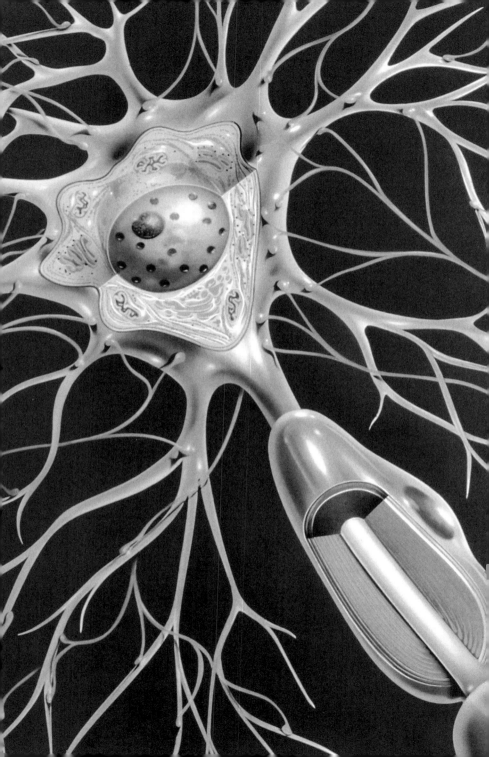

Mind Medicines and
the Nerves

When you think of mind medicines, also known as psychopharmaceuticals, think "receptors." Receptors are proteins on the surfaces of cells that are "turned on" when the right compound happens along. This receptor–activating molecule fits into the receptor much like a key fits into a lock. With the molecular key in place, the receptor protein changes shape and touches off a series of events inside the cell that eventually leads to a certain action inside the cell.

There are all kinds of receptors located on cells scattered throughout the body. For most receptors, compounds the body naturally produces, such as hormones or neurotransmitters, are supposed to fit into the "keyhole." What many psychopharmaceuticals do is interfere with receptors and alter the natural course of events. They can block receptors to inhibit a particular action, or they can switch them on, making the signal longer and stronger. Depending on the type of receptor or which type of neuron it is on, the effects of this manipulation can range from stimulation to sedation to euphoria. Fiddling with the receptors on your neurons can rev you up or calm you down.

The best way to understand psychopharmaceuticals, then, is to understand receptors, but to understand receptors it's important to know something about how neurons work. Sensory neurons gather information from the environment, which, after processing by the brain, is experienced in the form of sensations like cold or heat, sweet or sour, red or green. From this stream of sensory information, the brain must put together a clear picture of what is going on out in the world. Then, judgements on how best to respond to this information are formed and transmitted to muscles that control motion and speech. The brain manages this marvelous process by means of a complex network of neurons and the myriad connections they make with each other.

> Human neurons stained for better viewing.

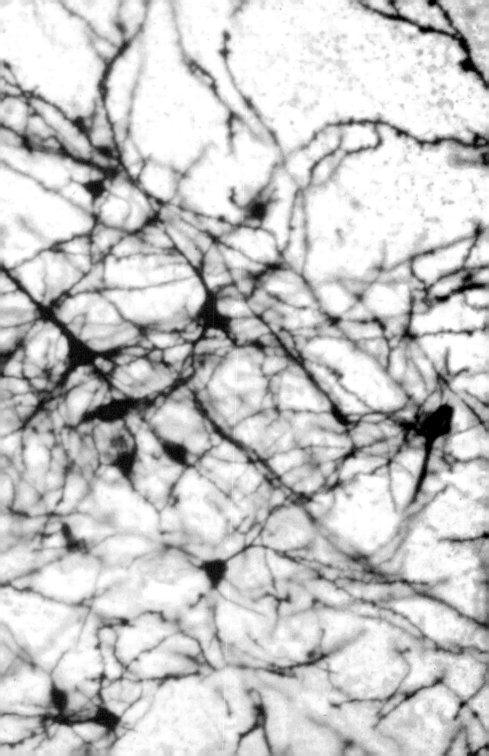

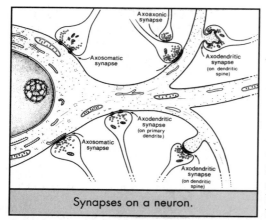

Synapses on a neuron.

The basic neuron is pretty much the same in all species of animals. What varies from one species to another is the number of neurons in the system, and the complexity of their interconnections. A lobster, for instance, gets by with a simple nervous system made up of just a few thousand neurons. But in the brain of the cunning human being, there are about 100 billion neurons, an astonishing amount, equal to the number of all the stars in our Galaxy. And each of these neurons is linked to an average of about 10,000 others, resulting in a massively intricate network with about 100 quadrillion connections.

In many ways, a neuron is a cell like any other in the body. Within the large cell of the neuron is its nucleus, containing DNA, the master genetic blueprint that controls the cell's internal workings. Neurons also have mitochondria, which produce cellular energy. What is unique to a neuron is its dendrites, which branch out from one end of the neuron to receive information from other neurons, and its axon, which projects from the other end of the cell and links it with other neurons.

The outer surface of a neuron, known as the membrane, is made up of a double layer of phospholipid. One end of phospholipid is hydrophobic, meaning it will not dissolve in water; the other end is hydrophilic and will readily dissolve in water. The hydrophobic tails of phospholipid turn inward to hide from the water that sur-

A lobster has only a few thousand neurons.

Our brain has as many neurons as our galaxy has stars.

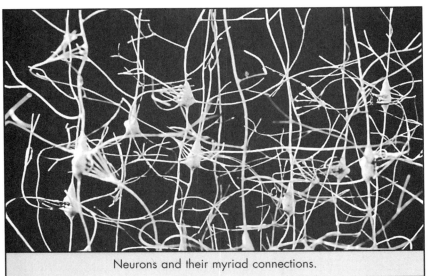

Neurons and their myriad connections.

rounds the cell, while the hydrophilic heads face outward. For the most part, the fatty membrane acts as a skin that seals out water-soluble molecules like sodium, potassium and many proteins. In order to communicate and to trade molecules with the outside world, a cell membrane has proteins, which are long chains of amino acids that are folded into various shapes depending on their function. These surface proteins float in the fatty membrane like icebergs, with much of their structures submerged within the membrane and only their peaks poking out into the outside environment or into the interior of the cell, or both. There are five basic types of proteins floating within the membrane:

Enzymes, which assemble or take apart molecules.

Structural elements, which provide the backbone and the glue that give a cell shape and attach it to other cells.

Pumps, which burn up energy as they pull in or pump out ions such as potassium, chloride or sodium.

Channels, which open or close to allow simple dissolved atoms like sodium and chloride—also known as ions—to flow in or out.

Receptors, which link up with signaling molecules like neurotransmitters and hormones to receive information from the outside world.

For mind medicines, it is the receptors, channels and pumps that are the most important proteins in the brain.

One essential difference between neurons and other cells is that neurons can communicate with each other directly and rapidly over great distances. Information is passed along the axon down to the synapse, a specialized point of connection with another neuron. Each neuron may receive inputs from thousands of other neurons via synapses. A neuron gets most of its input from synapses located on dendrites, although synapses also form on the axon or on the cell body.

Neurons are not actually attached to each other at the synapse; there is a microscopic gap between them. Information jumps that gap when neurotransmitters are released. Neurotransmitters are small molecules, such as acetylcholine, dopamine, and serotonin; they are stored in minute packages called vesicles and, when needed, are injected into the gap. Once released, they diffuse across to the neighboring neuron's synapse which has receptors specifically shaped to interact exclusively with each neurotransmitter. As noted above, the receptors are like locks

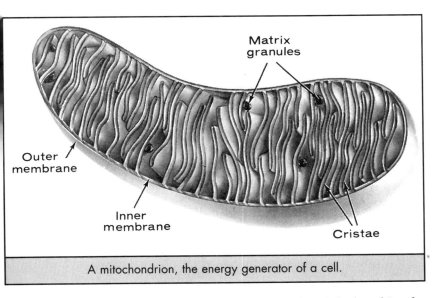

A mitochondrion, the energy generator of a cell.

and the neurotransmitters are like keys. When the right key hits the right lock, bingo, the receptor is turned on. Depending on what a specific receptor's job is, it can either excite a neuron, stimulating it to fire a message on down the chain, or it can calm the neuron, inhibiting its ability to pass along a message. As we'll see in the following chapters, many psychopharmaceuticals work by either blocking receptors or flooding them with excessive neurotransmitters.

Remember that a single neuron receives inputs from hundreds or thousands of other neurons, and the messages will be either inhibitory or excitatory. The neuron's job is to sort them all out. It is constantly taking a poll, and when the 'yes' votes—the excitatory signals—outnumber the 'no' votes—the inhibitory signals—it will fire a signal down along its own axon to the synapses adjacent to the next group of neurons.

The brain is not a computer, however, and axons are not wires. They do not transmit a signal down to the synapse with a jolt of electricity but by another method—an intriguing kind of chemistry. Just as you might keep the interior of your home lighter or darker, warmer or cooler than the outside environment, a neuron contains a fluid inside itself which is

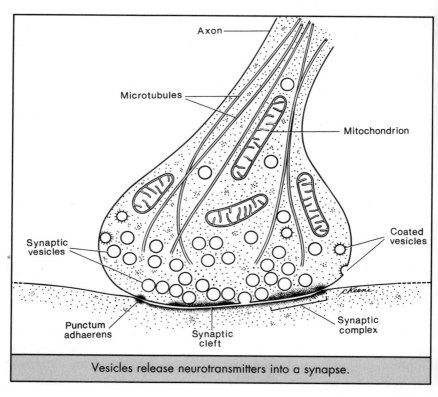

Axon

Microtubules

Mitochondrion

Coated vesicles

Synaptic vesicles

Punctum adhaerens

Synaptic cleft

Synaptic complex

Vesicles release neurotransmitters into a synapse.

quite different from that on the other side of the membrane. Pumps on the membrane constantly expel sodium ions, thus maintaining an exterior concentration of sodium that is about ten times higher than that found on the inside. It's as if there were fresh water inside the cell and salt water outside. There is an enormous number of these pumps—between a million and a billion for every square millimeter of cell membrane surface. Since sodium ions are positive, the difference in concentration of ions makes the inside of the cell electrically negative compared with the outside. The difference is tiny—equal to a mere 70 millivolts.

Along the length of the neuron's axon are channels that can suddenly pop open, allowing the sodium outside to rush in and change the electrical charge of the interior. When the neuron decides to fire off a signal, sodium channels at the top of the axon pop open. The sudden inrush of positively charged sodium ions causes an abrupt change in the internal charge of the cell. This rapid change, known as the action potential, triggers the next bunch of channels further downstream to pop open, and so on down the line until the wave of channel openings reaches the synapse. At this point, the synapse begins dumping neurotransmitters into the gap.

The axon is encased in an insulating substance called myelin. Every millimeter or so the myelin sheath is interrupted, which is where the sodium channels are found. Instead of spreading continuously down the axon, the action potential jumps from one gap to the next. Some nervous-system diseases, such as multiple sclerosis (MS), cause the myelin sheath to fall apart. Action potentials can not be effectively carried down the length of the axon, leading to problems with thought processing and motor control.

The action potential is an all-or-nothing sort of signal. A single nerve impulse causes the synapse to release only a given amount of a neurotransmitter. To pump up the "volume" of the signal, the neuron fires again and again and again, dumping more and more of the neurotransmitter into the synapse. The increased amount of neurotransmitter has a stronger effect on the downstream neuron, also known as the postsynaptic neuron. In between action-potential firings, the sodium pumps kick into high gear and expel sodium until the 70 millivolt difference between the inside and outside is achieved.

Meanwhile, down at the synaptic gap, neurotransmitters must be removed to clear the way for a new signal to get through. There are three ways they are cleared out: they drift out of range, they are disintegrated by enzymes or they are pumped back into the cell in a process called reuptake. In fact, many of the new antidepressant drugs, such as the much-discussed Prozac, actually block the pumps that suck serotonin back into the upstream neuron, also known as the presynaptic neuron. By blocking the reuptake of neurotransmitters from the synapse, transmission of certain nervous-system signals are significantly muted.

In the following chapter we will move on to the mind medicines themselves and look at how each one affects neurons.

The Mind
Medicines

The brain is a neurochemical engine. The speed and efficiency of the synaptic connections between neurons determines just how a certain part of the brain will function. Medicine can slow down a part of the brain that's overactive by revving up the release of inhibitory neurotransmitters, or it can speed up an underactive section by blocking the reuptake of excitatory neurotransmitters or by stimulating their release. The problem with mind medicines, both legal and illicit, is their side effects; that is, their tendency to activate too many different kinds of receptors, thus stimulating or suppressing parts of the brain other than the targeted areas. The key to improving psychopharmaceuticals lies in understanding more about exactly where each function of the brain occurs and developing compounds that target just one type of receptor in one very specific area of the brain.

It is important to remember that mind medicines do not "cure" mental illness; they simply allow the brain to function in a more normal way in spite of the underlying problems. For someone suffering from a debilitating and progressive disease such as schizophrenia, taking a drug can bring them back to the real world. For more background on specific mental illnesses, see chapter 6, but for now let's look at how the mind medicines affect neurons.

Medicines for Schizophrenia

It is still unclear what exactly is wrong with the brains of schizophrenics, but quite a bit is known about how the drugs used to counteract the disease affect neurons. *Rauwolfia serpentina* is a plant that has been known for centuries in India as an effective treatment for insomnia and insanity. Indian doctors in the 1930s discovered that extracts from this plant could also be used to treat high blood pressure, which inspired Ciba, a Swiss phar-

Rauwolfia serpentina.

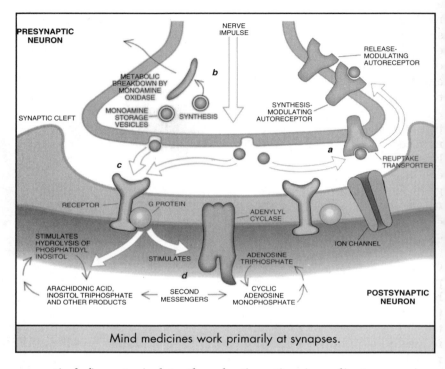

NERVE
IMPULSE

RELEASE-
MODULATING
AUTORECEPTOR

METABOLIC
BREAKDOWN BY
MONOAMINE
OXIDASE

b

SYNTHESIS-
MODULATING
AUTORECEPTOR

SYNAPTIC CLEFT

MONOAMINE
STORAGE
VESICLES

SYNTHESIS

a

REUPTAKE
TRANSPORTER

c

RECEPTOR

G PROTEIN

ADENYLYL
CYCLASE

ION CHANNEL

STIMULATES
HYDROLYSIS OF
PHOSPHATIDYL
INOSITOL

STIMULATES

ADENOSINE
TRIPHOSPHATE

d

ARACHIDONIC ACID,
INOSITOL TRIPHOSPHATE
AND OTHER PRODUCTS

SECOND
MESSENGERS

CYCLIC
ADENOSINE
MONOPHOSPHATE

POSTSYNAPTIC
NEURON

Mind medicines work primarily at synapses.

maceutical firm, to isolate the plant's active ingredient, reserpine. Because of India's long tradition of using *Rauwolfia serpentina* to alleviate insanity, reserpine was administered to schizophrenic patients in 1954 and was found to render them calmer and less suspicious.

This discovery had an enormous impact because it dovetailed with the identification by researchers of a number of the neurotransmitters active in the brain. What they eventually found was that reserpine reduces the levels of neurotransmitters. Another antipsychotic drug, originally developed in the early 1950s as an anesthetic, was chlorpromazine, later trade-named Thorazine. Both of these drugs were given to schizophrenic patients before it was clear exactly how they worked on the brain.

Eventually, it was found that the drugs block dopamine. Note that different types of neurons in different parts of the brain use different

neurotransmitters. Dopamine is a neurotransmitter that is used exten-
sively by the limbic system (see discussion in chapter 4), which apparently is dysfunctional in schizophrenia; the system's neurons seem to
dump too much dopamine into the synapses between neurons. An
antipsychotic drug like chlorpromazine blocks dopamine receptors on
the so-called postsynaptic neuron, located downstream of the synapse.
As it turns out, the drug's molecular structure is quite similar to the portion of the dopamine molecule that fits into the receptor. But chlorpromazine is not a perfect fit, and so it blocks the receptor without actually activating it. It's as if you have a bundle of keys, all meant for different locks from the same manufacturer. Any of the keys will fit into a
given lock, but only one will actually turn the cylinder. With chlorpromazine in the body, the dopamine receptors are blocked and the overactive limbic system slows down. Hallucinations often stop within days
and patients' concentration improves.

Stimulants like amphetamines and cocaine have the opposite effect
on the limbic system's dopamine receptor system. After an action
potential stimulates the release of dopamine, the presynaptic neuron
has proteins that will quickly pump the excess neurotransmitter out of
the gap to prepare for the next signal—this is the process called "reuptake." The neurotransmitter is thus recycled and is repackaged for later
release. Speed and coke block the reuptake of dopamine, and the neurons become overstimulated. Long-term, sufficiently high doses of
these drugs can cause the neurons to become so overexcited that the
limbic system breaks down, and psychotic symptoms very much like
schizophrenia emerge. In fact, many psychotic patients admitted on an
emergency basis to a psychiatric ward are not schizophrenic, but rather
are overdosing on crack or speed.

Antipsychotic drugs are helpful in treating schizophrenia, but they
are hardly miracle drugs. They aren't always effective and can cause serious side effects. Chlorpromazine and similar drugs will cause tardive
dyskinesia in 13 percent of chronic schizophrenic patients who use them.
This syndrome consists of repetitive involuntary movements of the
mouth and tongue, such as chewing, sucking, and smacking the lips. The
arms, legs and even the whole body can begin jerking. It's a frightening
side effect that sometimes does not disappear even when the drugs are
halted. Clozapine is a new antipsychotic drug that also blocks dopamine,

"The Scream" by Edvard Munch.

but in a different part of the brain from that affected by the other drugs, and it doesn't appear to touch off tardive dyskinesia. Even this improved antipsychotic drug has problems, however; it can cause white blood cell levels to plummet in about two percent of patients who take it.

Schizophrenia is primarily a brain illness and drug therapy is the principal treatment. But because drugs cannot teach the life and coping skills needed to handle the stresses of the real world, psychotherapy also plays a role. One type of therapy, supportive therapy, seems to be particularly useful in teaching patients how to deal with the practical problems of living with a debilitating disease (see chapter 7 for details).

Medicines for Mania and Depression

Lithium

The first medicine developed especially for bipolar disorder was lithium, a simple metallic element that is a close relative of sodium and potassium, which are themselves abundantly present in cells. Lithium is not normally found in appreciable amounts in the body, however. In 1948, John Cade, an Australian psychiatrist, was trying to determine if there was a toxic agent that manic patients were excreting into their urine that would explain their condition. His method of hunting for this brain poison was to inject urine from manic patients into guinea pigs and observe the effects. At one point, instead of injecting raw urine, he decided to switch to solutions made up

Depression can lead to drug overdose.

of the major constituents of urine, like urea and uric acid. He faced a problem in making up these solutions, though, since uric acid does not dissolve very easily in water. By luck, he used a highly soluble form of uric acid, a powder called lithium urate, to make up the solution. He found that the guinea pigs injected with the new solution became profoundly lethargic. Later he discovered that it was the lithium in the solution, not the uric acid, that was responsible for de-energizing the test rodents. He moved quickly on to humans and decided to try out lithium on a 51-year-old man who had been chronically manic for five years. This man was, as Cade wrote, "amiably restless, dirty, destructive, mischievous and interfering." He further wrote that the subject "enjoyed preeminent nuisance value in a back ward for all those years and bid fair to remain there for the rest of his life."

Within three weeks of beginning treatment with lithium, the man snapped out of his mania and was moved out of the back ward into the convalescent ward. Three months later, he was discharged from the hospital. Unfortunately, lithium did not come into general use in the U.S. until 1971, partly because it had previously been tried out as a cardiac drug, killed several patients, and was withdrawn from the market. That lithium works is not in doubt, but nobody seems to have a clear idea of why it works. Unlike antipsychotic drugs that target specific neurotransmitter receptors, lithium finds its way into every cell in the body. Sorting out exactly where it is having its effect is a very tricky business.

Scientists do know that lithium blocks the action of an enzyme known as inositol phosphatase. This enzyme plays a role in the cascade of biochemical changes that take place after a receptor is turned on by a neurotransmitter. By analogy, when the key (a receptor) is turned to start a car (a neuron), a contact is closed at the ignition switch which in turn causes the starter to rotate and high voltage electricity to flow through the ignition coil, the distributor and the spark plugs. Lithium interrupts the flow of juice to the starter, making the car hard to start. In other words, the neurons are sedated, and less inclined to fire, and the manic symptoms are brought under control. Also, for some unknown reason, lithium not only makes the highs less high, it also makes the lows less low. Sometimes, lithium by itself isn't enough to counteract the depressions, and antidepressant drugs (discussed below) are given along with it.

Lithium has its problems, most notably that it fails to work for about a third of the people who take it. It is least effective in patients with mixed moods, where euphoria and depression are occurring at the same time, and in cases of rapid cycling, where cycles of highs and lows happen four or more times a year. Even among those who find lithium helpful and use it faithfully, 60 percent will still have another manic outburst.

Recently, researchers have discovered that drugs used to prevent epileptic seizures, such as valproic acid, can also break the cycle of bipolar disorder. What is fascinating about this drug is that it interacts with the GABA receptor, the same receptor that alcohol and barbiturate drugs act upon. More details on the critical GABA receptor can be found below in the discussion of antianxiety drugs.

Antidepressants

In the case of major depressions, antidepressants are used, and the ways in which these chemicals affect neurons are pretty well known. Each one changes the way neurotransmitters are taken up by receptors, or the way they are broken down. The newest class of antidepressants such as Prozac and Zoloft selectively blocks the reuptake of the neurotransmitter serotonin, which is frequently used by neurons involved in emotion. This reuptake blocking boosts the serotonin signal to the postsynaptic neurons, which relieves depression. The difficulty lies in trying to figure out how something happening at the level of synapses gets built into a complex behavior like depression.

Remember, though, that the brain is composed of different types of neurons and each type has its own favorite neurotransmitters. Those neurons involved in determining mood predominantly use serotonin, so that by affecting levels of serotonin, mood can be altered.

A common medical practice is for psychiatrists to take their patients off antidepressant drugs once the symptoms of depression have abated, on the theory that the patients have been cured or stabilized. This practice was especially prevalent in the days when the only drugs for depression were tricyclic antidepressants and monoamine oxidase inhibitors. The tricyclics, so called because they have three rings of carbon in their chemical structure, block the reuptake of several neurotransmitters, not just serotonin. Consequently, they have more effects on more neurons, which means they have more side effects than do the newer antidepressants.

But new studies have shown that major depression should be considered a long-term disease with a high probability of reoccurrence. The research indicates that patients who stay on antidepressants have a much lower incidence of falling into a depressed state again. And with new drugs available that have fewer side effects, it is now more feasible to stay on antidepressants much longer. Fewer side effects also means that antidepressants can be used by people who are mildly or moderately depressed. However, as will be discussed in chapter 9, the use of the new antidepressants has spread much farther than is perhaps desirable, and into areas that are inappropriate, such as promoting weight loss.

Drugs are not the only effective approach in treating depression. Antidepressants are certainly useful but so is psychotherapy, either in combination with drugs or by itself. See chapter 7 for more details on psychotherapies. But if depression is only an organic disease why is it responsive to talk therapy? Some researchers think that the confusion arises because there are really two types of major depression—one is almost exclusively caused by disordered brain chemistry and the other can be touched off in susceptible individuals by life difficulties. As psychiatrist Wayne Drevets of the Washington University School of Medicine has said, "If you've got one of these severe types of depression that we've studied, you can't just pull yourself up by your bootstraps and shape up without proper drug treatment." Milder forms of depression can often be dealt with without resorting to psychopharmaceuticals.

Electroconvulsive Therapy

For the severest forms of depression, the treatment of last resort is electroconvulsive therapy (ECT), also called shock therapy because it involves applying an electric jolt to the brain. It is perhaps best known as the gruesome treatment employed in the movie *One Flew Over the Cuckoo's Nest*, where it was used by a sadistic nurse to subdue or punish patients. The movie was not far off the mark; in the past, ECT was often misused or overused in some large or understaffed institutions. Nowadays, however, it is used quite sparingly and far more humanely, with lower voltages applied to the brain and muscle relaxants adminis-

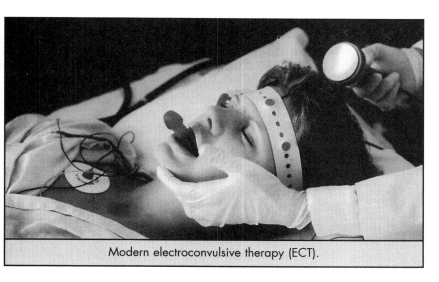
Modern electroconvulsive therapy (ECT).

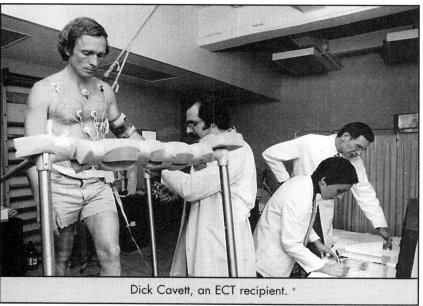
Dick Cavett, an ECT recipient.

tered to reduce the risk of a convulsing patient breaking a bone. The pulses of electricity cause small seizures in the brain, not unlike those experienced by epileptics, and this seems to somehow restore the balance of neurotransmitters in the brain that are linked to mood. But given the profound number of biochemical changes that an induced seizure has on the brain, it has been difficult to sort out exactly what is responsible for ECT's success in snapping deeply depressed patients out of their illness.

ECT is a more widespread therapy than one might imagine. About 30,000 Americans undergo the procedure each year; among them talk-show host Dick Cavett. "ECT was miraculous," Cavett said in a 1992 *People* magazine article. "My wife was dubious, but when she came into my room afterward, I sat up and said, 'Look who's back among the living.' It was like a magic wand."

Despite Cavett's glowing endorsement of the procedure, ECT can have serious side effects. It often fails to lift the depression, and whether it's effective or not, it can cause confusion and significant memory loss. Critics of the procedure say it is really the memory loss itself that lifts depression, not some mysterious restoration of neurochemical balance. It "works" because the memory loss is so profound that patients cannot remember why they are depressed, according to ECT critics.

The memory loss can be extensive. Some ECT recipients find they cannot remember events from as far back as six months before their treatment. As a result, ECT is used sparingly today.

Dealing with Anxiety States

What do alcohol, anticonvulsants and antianxiety drugs all have in common? They work through the GABA receptor. GABA stands for gamma-aminobutyric acid, which is an inhibitory neurotransmitter. As we have already learned, neurons can either excite the postsynaptic neuron, that is, they tend to stimulate an action potential, or they inhibit the neuron, meaning they suppress firing.

GABA-releasing neurons are what you might think of as the brain's brake system. When GABA is released at a synapse it migrates to the postsynaptic neuron's GABA receptors. These proteins are not just receptors, they are also chloride channels. Channels are proteins that allow ions to freely flow through them when open. Also, between firings, the interior of a neuron is brought down to –70 millivolts through the vigorous work of sodium pumps. The action potential passes down a neuron when sodium channels pop open and the highly concentrated, positively charged sodium ions flood in.

It turns out that chloride ions are also highly concentrated outside of a neuron, and as with sodium, there are chloride pumps and chloride channels. Many types of chloride channels are sensitive to GABA. When this neurotransmitter

Coffee beans, a source of caffeine.

is released by a presynaptic neuron and inserts itself into the GABA receptor, the chloride channel springs open. The chloride ions pour in, but owing to their negative charges, they actually make the cell even more negative than usual. This inrush of chloride drops the internal charge of the neuron even further, to about –80 millivolts. This means the neuron is that much more resistant to firing off an action potential. For the neuron, it's like trying to drive uphill with the brake on.

What antianxiety drugs do is to increase the potency of the response to GABA. Drugs like Valium lock onto these chloride channels right next to GABA, but when both of them are present at the same time, the channels open wider and longer, thus doubling the amount of chloride flowing into the cell. Using the brake analogy once again, antianxiety drugs are like a power assist to the chloride channel. For the neuron, it's now like driving uphill with the parking brake on, making it even harder to fire off an action potential.

Anxiety.

As noted above, different types of neurons use different neurotransmitters. Antianxiety drugs only work on neurons that take up GABA as a transmitter. However, there are many different types of GABA receptors. There are GABA receptors not only in neurons involved in producing anxiety, but also in neurons that control muscles. Valium and alcohol both seem to potentiate GABA receptors in the part of the brain that deals with anxiety, but alcohol adversely affects other parts of the brain, causing stumbling, wobbling and stammering, which make it an undesirable antianxiety drug.

To avoid side effects, neuroscientists choose or design drugs that are specific, that is, they interact only with the right receptors on the right sorts of neurons. But finding that right receptor and neuron out in the dense forest of 100 billion neurons is extremely difficult, even with new highly effective brain-scanning technology. The effort to design new and improved mind medicines is still mostly a hit-or-miss process. Often, when a new drug is found that "works," it is used even when its mechanisms are not clearly understood. Later, neuroscientists try to find out why it works, and to create variations that do the job better or with greater precision.

Drugs of Abuse

Alcohol and other addictive drugs produce their intoxicating effects in much the same ways as do the prescription medicines described above. As we've already seen, alcohol seems to produce euphoria and intoxication by binding to the GABA receptor, which doubles its activity and slows down the anxiety center of the brain.

Amphetamines, such as methamphetamine, also affect dopamine-using neurons. These compounds actually get inside the neuron and stimulate the presynaptic vesicles—those tiny spheres that hold neurotransmit-

Rats also seek drug "rewards."

Why do you think they call it dope?

Illegal psychopharmaceuticals.

ters—to spill dopamine into the synapse, even when no action potential has ordered this release. Both cocaine and amphetamines produce a net increase in the amount of dopamine found in the synapse. As far as the user is concerned, the effects of smoking methamphetamine or crack cocaine are so similar it is hard to tell the difference. However, methamphetamine's stimulating effects are longer-lasting. This stimulation elevates one's mood—it gets one "high"—and people high on cocaine report feeling invincible and indestructible. Cocaine appeals primarily to people who are already up, as a way of maintaining and augmenting their normal state. According to Stanford Medical Center psychiatrist Dr. Roy King, "If you're highly extroverted, even slightly manic, by temperament, cocaine augments your natural high."

Caffeine is the most widely used mind medicine, with more than 92 percent of adults in America regularly consuming it in tea, coffee or cola. This stimulant works by blocking the receptors for another inhibitory neurotransmitter, adenosine. This neurotransmitter acts as a kind of brake on the release of glutamate, which is an excitatory neurotransmitter. Caffeine essentially releases the brake on glutamate, and the more you take the less braking action there is. One desirable effect is that it speeds up mental processes and in particular stimulates the attention-focusing center of the brain. An undesirable side effect is that the absence of the adenosine brake overexcites motor neurons; that is, you get the shakes.

PCP, originally developed as a surgical anesthetic, is no longer legally sold in the U.S. because it has such strong hallucinogenic properties. Like Valium, PCP works on an ion channel, but in this case the channel controls the entry into the neuron of calcium ions. Glutamate is found throughout the brain and when it binds to a calcium channel it allows these ions to flow in, and this inrush of calcium excites the neuron, making it more likely to fire off an action potential. PCP blocks glutamate from turning on these calcium channels, which results not only in the blockage of pain transmission but also can produce distorted perception, i.e., hallucinations.

Opiates like morphine and heroin work quite differently from the stimulants. They bind to the receptors used by the body's natural opiates. These natural opiates, called endorphins and enkephalins, are peptides made up of strings of from five to 30 amino acids. Longer strings of amino acids are generally called proteins.

Endorphins and enkephalins have a number of natural functions in the brain. They are released in response to injury or during a state of panic, or even during exertion such as long-distance running; they may be responsible for what is known as "runner's high." Neurons within the brain that are involved in the perception of pain, for instance, have receptors on their cell surfaces for these substances. When they are turned on by the natural opiates, the transmission of pain is turned way down, through an internal neuronal process that is not well understood. Morphine and its more potent cousin, heroin, have molecular structures that resemble critical areas of the endorphin and enkephalin molecules and will also turn on the pain-suppressing receptors. Besides simply relieving pain, both the natural and artificial opiates act on other neurons to produce euphoria. The peptides themselves are not administered as drugs because they are easily broken down by enzymes in the blood or intestine, and they cannot easily penetrate the thick, restrictive membranes—known as the blood-brain barrier—which blocks the entry of many potentially toxic substances. Morphine and heroin are not broken down as easily and do indeed cross the blood-brain barrier.

The Addiction System

Addiction to a drug, whether it be to heroin, cocaine or nicotine, happens in a process quite separate from mere physical habituation. A drug user becomes physically addicted to a drug when the body adapts to being constantly bathed in a substance. For instance, when excessive levels of dopamine are always present in a synapse because of cocaine abuse, it will respond by making fewer receptors on the postsynaptic side. Imagine that your neighbor makes a constant habit of playing loud music, so you shut your window. Because the noise is so loud, you can still hear it. But if the neighbor suddenly turns down the volume—which is analogous to stopping a drug—you won't hear a thing. Your neurons are not windows, however, and cannot simply be yanked back open. When drugs are suddenly stopped it takes several days for the dopamine receptors to be reestablished and get back to normal.

Physical addiction is not the key to hard-core drug addiction, however. Remember, the brain is a marvelously complex parallel-distributed processing organ, and there is always more going on than meets the eye. Drug addicts, alcoholics and even cigarette smokers who are dried out or detoxified will, in most cases, go right back to their habits. The only difference is they will initially need far less of the drug to get high than before detoxification.

Where the action is really happening is in the reward system of the brain. Eating, drinking, having sex and nurturing offspring are all essential to the survival of the human race. To insure that you do these things on a regular basis, or at least try to, the brains of humans and other mammals have evolved a set of interconnected neurons that are specifically designed to provide pleasure as a reward. This reward system—called the mesocorticolimbic pathway (MCLP)—is connected to many brain parts. It is primarily located in the limbic system, an area of the brain that is also involved in emotion. Addicting drugs activate the reward system in such a way that users begin to see drug use as an indispensable activity like eating and drinking. Just as they would if deprived of food, addicts experience pain and suffering when they are starved for their drug, and they experience a rush of pleasure when they feed their craving. They have taught their reward system to desire a new substance, and again, simply weaning an addict from a drug does not break this learned pattern.

Some people seem to be particularly prone to having their reward system hijacked by addicting drugs, and researchers suspect that there are powerful genetic forces at work. However, the precise gene or genes involved have yet to be located. Drug and alcohol addicts have a terrible track record for relapse. At best, only a 50 percent long-term cure rate can be expected and that only when extremely coercive measures are used.

There are no effective drugs to counteract the addict's craving, although antabuse can help alcoholics avoid drinking. For most other drugs, some forms of counseling have been shown to be at least somewhat effective, in particular cognitive-behavioral therapy, which will be discussed in chapter 7.

Blocking the Drinking Impulse

Antabuse is a potentially lethal drug used to help alcoholics keep from drinking. The drug doesn't affect the GABA receptors that alcohol interacts with to produce euphoria and tipsiness. Instead, antabuse blocks the enzymes in the liver that metabolize alcohol. As a result, a toxic compound called acetaldehyde builds up in the body. After a single drink, the built-up acetaldehyde produces flushing, throbbing in the head, and breathing difficulty. If the drinking goes on, it can even cause death. Antabuse does not stop the craving for liquor, but through its negative effects it does make it easier to resist temptation.

The Brain

he 100 billion neurons in the brain are connected with one another in marvelous and intricate ways that make vision, movement, learning, memory and thought possible. Remarkably, as the brain of an unborn child develops, few of the trillions of connections between the billions of neurons are present. The parts of the brain and the individual neurons first grow as bundles of cells; the wiring up of this complex is dealt with next.

Reaching Out

Like leaves stretching toward sunlight, the dendrites of a neuron grow outward in search of the right axons, and like tap roots, axons grope around until they link up with the neurons designated to receive their output. Neurons are incredibly precise in finding the right "address" and hooking up the correct wiring.

Before neurons can send out axons and dendrites, they have to establish residency somewhere in the brain, spinal cord or elsewhere in the body. During the first few weeks of development, when the human embryo still looks something like a question-mark-shaped worm, new neurons are formed in a dark little stripe of tissue called the neural tube. On the inner surface of the tube are neurons whose sole job is to divide and give birth to other neurons. Newborn neurons must then crawl along ladder-like fibers emanating from support cells, called glial cells. The earliest-born neurons tend to stay at the bottom; the later ones move up to the top. The end result is anywhere from three to five layers of neurons, with each layer having different functions. The top layer tends to receive input; those further down process information and create appropriate outputs.

Once the neurons are in place, the dividing cells that gave birth to them die off. From then on, no more neurons are born. While severed axons can often regenerate if cut or can form new synapses, once an entire neuron dies, it cannot be replaced. Brain and spinal-cord damage

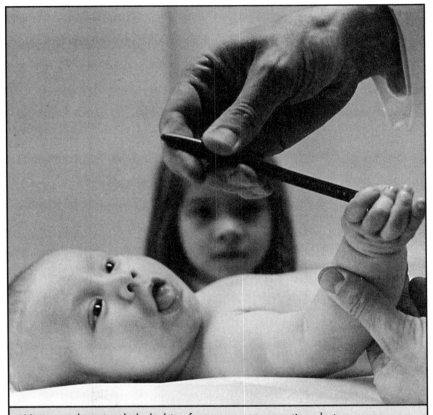

Vision and motion help babies form proper connections between neurons.

Lou Gehrig says farewell to baseball.

and diseases that cause neurons to degenerate are so devastating because, unlike injuries to skin, muscle and bone, profound nervous-system damage cannot readily be repaired.

When you were born, you already had about all the neurons you will ever have, even though your infant brain only weighed about a fourth of your adult brain. Your brain grows not because more neurons are formed but because those already in place get larger and because the number of axons and dendrite connections increases.

Making Connections

When all the neurons are in place in the developing brain, the daunting task of "wiring" the system is next. The process of making synaptic connections is something like stringing telephone wires between two houses in different cities. To string wires between houses in New York and Washington, DC, say, you have to bypass Philadelphia, Baltimore and several smaller cities. Once in Washington, the lines have to be routed to the right neighborhood and finally to the correct address. There are no maps or signs to guide neurons in their quest to make the right connection; instead, they follow biochemical signals.

Axons and dendrites generally begin to grow out from the newborn neuron soon after the cell reaches its final location. The guidance system is contained in an enlargement at the tip of an axon or dendrite called a growth cone. The growth cone both drives forward movement and steers the axon as it gropes its way through the surrounding forest of neurons at an excruciatingly slow rate of a millimeter a day. The growth cone looks something like a hand with a broad, flat expansion like a palm that has many long microspikes extending outward like fingers. These microspikes are constantly probing about, exploring for bio-chemical clues that protrude from the surfaces of surrounding cells and tell it which route to take. When microspikes make contact with an unfavorable surface, they shrink back, and when they find a favorable surface, they attach and pull the growth cone in that direction. When the growth cone of an axon finally reaches its destination, it hooks up by forming a synapse with the target cell, usually on one of the den-drites, but they can also attach to the cell body or to the axon of the tar-get neuron. Out in the peripheral nervous system, neurons form synapses with muscle cells or with sensory cells in the eyes, ears, nose, tongue or skin.

Since more neurons cannot be made on demand, the body creates far more than are necessary. It then weeds them out, something akin to a lumberjack thinning out an overgrown forest. The body makes about twice as many neurons as it needs, and to survive, neurons must com-pete for neurotrophic factors, which are proteins that send a "stay alive" message to the cell. The target cell produces only so much of these neurotrophic factors and portions them out primarily to the axons it wants to retain. As in a large litter of puppies, all trying to get their share of a limited supply of mother's milk, the runts will die off. Neurons that do not suck up enough of the neurotrophic factor from their axons self-destruct in a process called programmed cell death.

Even after the thinning process is over, neurons continue to depend on neurotrophic factors to stay alive. Today, researchers at biotechnol-ogy and pharmaceutical companies are attempting to reverse or halt the effects of such neurodegenerative conditions as Lou Gehrig's dis-ease by supplying the nerves with extra doses of these life-giving neu-rotrophic factors.

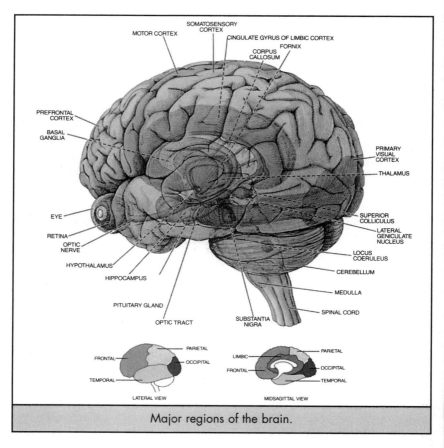

Major regions of the brain.

The Parts of the Brain

As neurons are born, sort themselves out and then form connections, the central nervous system (CNS) grows and divides itself into six major areas with quite distinct functions.

The spinal cord is the simplest part of the CNS. It extends from the base of the skull, passing through the hollow middle of the vertebrae. The spinal cord contains neurons that connect to the peripheral nervous system. The peripheral nervous system is formed by neurons that are located mainly outside the spinal cord or brain. They are the neurons that transmit sensory information from joints, muscles and skin. As information about the environment and the position of the body flows upward to the brain, signals pass downward through a different set of neurons and out to muscles which translate the information into motion.

Moving upwards from the spinal cord, the next area is the brain stem. The cranial nerves originate in the brain stem and extend out into various locations in the head, to the tongue, nose, ears and facial skin; they also control the muscles of the face. The brain stem consists of two parts: the medulla helps controls some basic body functions such as blood pressure and breathing, and the pons relays information from the cerebral hemispheres above to the cerebellum.

The cerebellum is wrapped around the back of the brain stem and is involved in some fairly basic functions. The cerebellum receives sensory input from the muscles and movement information from the cerebral cortex and coordinates muscle movements.

Perched atop the brain stem is the midbrain, which plays a major role in controlling eye movements, and also acts as a relay for hearing and visual inputs. The thalamus and hypothalamus are sandwiched between the cerebral hemispheres. In this region, sensory information—except for sight and smell, which are directly relayed to the brain—is processed before passing on to the cerebral cortex. Emotional responses seem to originate here, and the autonomic nervous system, which governs heart rate, breathing and such, is also controlled here.

These parts of the brain have little to do with the conscious part of our world, what we call "thought." Rather, these are the automatic portions of the brain that can be found just as readily in a bird, a crocodile or a mouse. What sets the human brain apart from other species is the impressive amount of neural material found in the cerebral hemispheres. The topmost layer of these hemispheres, sometimes called the "grey matter," looks in cross-section so much like the bark of a tree that it is called the cortex, which is the Latin word for bark. The cortex is where the powerful neurons that do the work of thought, movement and vision reside. Underneath the cortex layer is the cerebrum, often called the "white matter" because it is composed of bundles of white, glistening axons connecting various regions of the cortex with other parts of the brain.

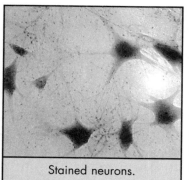

Stained neurons.

During the course of evolution, the human cerebral cortex grew in size faster than did the skull, resulting in a tightly folded structure that allows more of this grey matter to be stuffed in. A rat's tiny brain has a bit of cerebral cortex, but it is not particularly folded. The cat's cerebral cortex is larger than the rat's and is folded to some extent. So it's the crafty cat with the larger cerebral cortex that catches the rat, not vice versa. Among mammals, the human brain has the highest degree of folding and the greatest amount of cortex devoted to higher-order thinking. The frontal lobes are far larger in humans than in even our closest primate relative, the chimpanzee.

Each part of the cortex is devoted to distinct functions. The wide stripe of the cortex that wraps up and over the brain like a saddle is devoted to the sense of touch. The adjacent area governs voluntary muscle movement. Movement of various body parts is assigned to very specific locations within that stripe. Your toes, for instance, are controlled by the topmost part of the stripe. Further along the stripe are control areas for your ankles, knees, hips, trunk, shoulders, elbows, wrists and hands. The fingers have a considerable amount of the cortex devoted to them. Facial expressions also occupy a disproportionately large number of neurons. The visual cortex is tucked away at the very back of the brain.

Language and speaking functions are found along the side of the brain in the temporal lobes. Speech provides an ideal example of what is known as distributed processing. Rather than thought and speech happening together in a single part of the brain, thoughts are first formed in the frontal lobe and must pass through the language area and then on to the motor control areas of the cortex to result in spoken words.

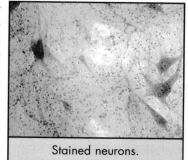

Stained neurons.

Bird Brains Grow New Memories

In the fall, when the trees drop their load of leaves onto the ground, the sky grows grey and the insects begin to die off, the black-capped chickadee must stash away seeds and nuts to last it through winter's chill. When the time comes, the chickadee has to remember exactly where it buried those seeds. For a lot of us humans, simply remembering where we put our wallet, glasses or car keys can be a real challenge, and this is with one of the largest brains in the animal world. In the chickadee, whose body must be as tiny and light as possible in order to fly, the brain must be minuscule and as a result is unsophisticated.

The solution for the chickadee is to add more neurons on demand. The bird's hippocampus—a portion of the brain critical to memory storage and spatial learning—swells in size every October. Old neurons with last year's memories die off and new neurons are born. It's as if a notebook full of scribblings is thrown away and a new one is bought to jot down this year's notes.

The chickadee is not the only bird that can grow new memories. Songbirds, such as the canary, also discard old neurons and grow new ones in order to learn the season's latest version of its characteristic song.

Chickadees and songbirds seem to be exceptions to the general rule that adult animals never produce new neurons. Human brains do not appear to ever grow new neurons and so we must be content with our memories the way they are.

Reading the Bumps

More than a century ago, the German physician Franz Joseph Gall dedicated his life to the study of the brain. He introduced a curious science that he called phrenology. He and his disciples believed that 37 different character traits, such as cautiousness and aggressiveness, each had their own unique location in the brain. And Gall thought that by measuring the size of the bumps on the skull, he could get a pretty good indication of how active and advanced the underlying brain tissue was. In 1802, religious authorities in Vienna took a dim view of Gall's phrenology because it implied that character traits were "hardwired" and couldn't be changed by prayer and religious education. Banished from Austria, he nonetheless persevered and spread his ideas across Europe and to America where physicians at first embraced it. Walt Whitman and Edgar Allen Poe were among those fascinated by phrenology. In time, phrenology fell into disrepute and came to be regarded in the same light as tea-leaf reading and crystal-ball gazing. Still, Gall was on to something. He was the first to propose that different attributes of the mind are located in different parts of the brain, although bump size has nothing to do with the underlying brain matter. Today, neuroscientists analyze sophisticated images from PET and MRI scans—not the bumps on your head—to observe changes taking place in your brain as you think, talk, speak and walk.

Much of what we call "thinking" is accomplished in the frontal cortex. And much of the disordered thinking associated with schizophrenia seems to happen up front. The prefrontal lobotomy, a crude operation by modern standards, was performed on patients from the 1930s to the 1950s to eliminate psychotic, often violent behavior. But the procedure wiped out much of the intellect, too.

The limbic system lies underneath the cortex in the center of the

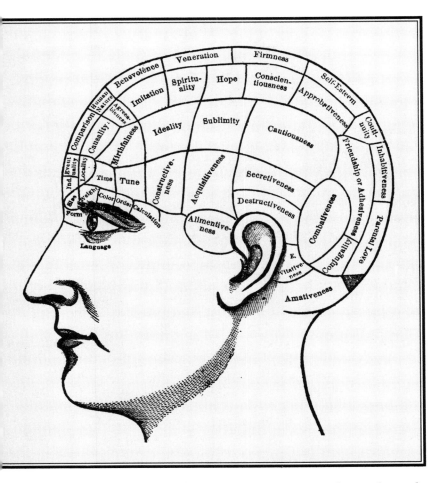

brain. It used to be thought of as an unimportant area devoted mostly to the sense of smell. But it turns out the limbic system is connected to practically every part of the brain, and it plays a central role in the expression of emotion.

As we move on in our tour of the brain, in the next two chapters we will explore how the brain and mind work when they are well in order to better understand what goes wrong in mental illness.

From Brain
to Mind

The visual system is perhaps the most complex of all our senses and provides a beautiful illustration of how the billions of diffuse neurons coalesce to form the mind. While the auditory nerve that carries sound signals from the ear to the brain has about 30,000 axons, the optic nerve is a thick bundle with about a million axons. Since vision is very important to our survival, the brain has dedicated an entire separate region, located at the back and called the occipital lobes, to process the visual signals.

While the eye can in some ways be compared to a camera, the brain is definitely not like film. It doesn't passively receive the visual signal; rather, it extracts several different kinds of images from your eyes. And these images are optimized to give the most information about, for example, shape and motion, or color, or depth and texture.

Light passes through the cornea, which like a camera lens focuses the image onto the retina. Light is then converted into nerve impulses by specialized sensory neurons called photoreceptors. These light-sensitive neurons come in two varieties: rods and cones. Because rods are cylindrical and much longer than cones, they are especially well adapted to capturing every bit of light energy that falls upon them. So they are indispensable for night vision, but that is about all. If you lost all of the rods in your eye, the result would be night blindness, but in daylight you would hardly notice the loss.

More important are the cones, which are less sensitive to light but which detect color. One kind of cone is most sensitive to red, another to green and a third to blue. The brain blends the three separate color signals to decide what the color really is. If your brain receives an equal amount of nerve impulses from red-sensitive cones as from blue-sensitive cones, it will probably decide that the color you're seeing is purple.

Color blindness results when a person is born with a defect in one of

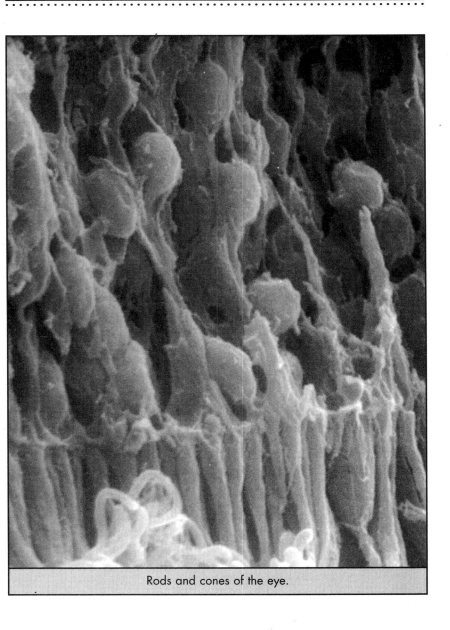

Rods and cones of the eye.

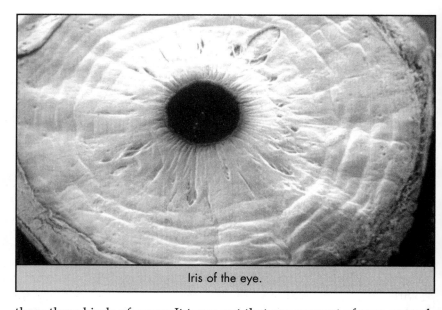

Iris of the eye.

these three kinds of cones. It turns out that one percent of men are red-blind and another two percent are green-blind. Color blindness is a mutation, in which the genes that code for light-sensitive pigments are seriously altered. These pigments, which are proteins embedded in photoreceptors, change shape when struck by light of the right color. In mutated forms, certain critical amino acids are awry and pigment proteins no longer flex properly. As a result, they don't set off the chain of events that results in a nerve impulse. More men are afflicted with color blindness than women, for one simple reason. The genes for red and green pigments are on the X chromosome. Since men get only one X chromosome—the other being a Y—and women receive two Xs, if a man's X has a mutated gene on it, he is out of luck because there is no other X to provide a backup copy. Women, with their two Xs, usually have a functional backup on their other X. Rarely, a woman will get the bad gene on both Xs and will of course also become color blind.

Vision is critically important for our survival. Our brains need to extract a great deal of information from this sensory system. The visual image you "see" in your mind is not simply the output of each photoreceptor hardwired into the back of your brain. Instead, the signal is broken into different types of "maps" that wire into their own special areas of the occipital lobes. When these images are recombined in a sophisticated way, the brain forms the rich, colorful, three-dimensional view of the world from what really is just a two-dimensional set of dots on the back of the eye.

Forming separate maps for different tasks—a process referred to as parallel processing—begins right in the retina. Certain neurons, called ganglion cells, interact with photoreceptors. Large ganglion cells add together the signals from the cones to produce a black-and-white image with the greatest possible signal strength. Small ganglion cells keep the outputs from the different types of cones separated and pass along the color information to the brain. Axons from both large and small ganglion cells bunch together to form the optic nerve, which converges on the thalamus, a part of the brain that is like the Grand Central Station of sensory information.

Axons from the retinal neurons do not simply connect with the thalamus randomly. They plug into the thalamus following the pattern that is wired into the retina. It's as if the neurons project the image from the eyes onto the thalamus. The black-and-white and color images remain separated, though, and project onto separate parts of the thalamus. When the visual images make their next jump—this time to the back of the brain—they remain separated. The visual signals are then broken down still further once they arrive in the brain. The occipital lobes, at the back of the brain, have six distinct areas onto which various versions of the retinal image are projected. Imagine having six different computers installed, each one tapping into the same information stream—more or less—and each running a different program. Yet they are all cabled together so they can share information.

The separate visual images are processed to achieve different goals. One area receives its inputs from large ganglion neurons, which add up all the color images into black and white dots. This area receives information most rapidly, in what amounts to a grainy photocopy of the retinal image minus such niceties as color and texture, which are essential to recognizing and identifying an object. This part of the visual system simply wants to know if an object is in motion. Such information is vital if, for instance, a tiger is lunging at you or someone is swinging a club

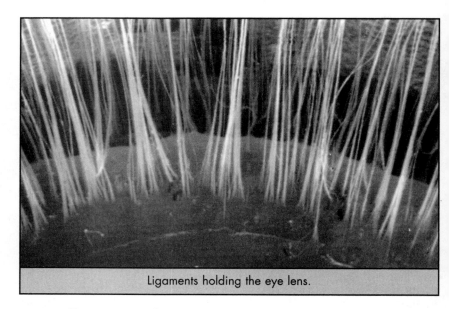

Ligaments holding the eye lens.

at you. Processing information takes time, so the brain first sends sketchy visual information to what is essentially a motion detector.

Motion is so important to us that we often perceive movements before we even know what we've seen. From the visual scene, the brain can instantly snatch out a shadowy bit of a moving image, determine its direction, and make a guess as to whether it poses a threat. This allows our fight-or-flight reflex to kick in even before we know what it is we're fighting or fleeing from. The brain saves a lot of time with this motion detector. It takes just 75 milliseconds to process an image for purposes of detecting motion, but it takes another 100 milliseconds for your brain to make a positive I.D. So the motion-detector function cuts your reaction time by more than half.

Motion detection is a special case, however. The larger task of vision is to provide a rich, three-dimensional image and to recognize major elements in the image. To do this, the brain combines several of the images projected onto the back of the brain. Some image-processing areas specialize in defining sharp edges; others are expert at recognizing and assigning colors. All of this happens in the so-called preconscious part of your brain, so you do not have to "think" about images and make decisions about whether that color is green or that object is square. But to recognize an object as a leaf or a box, the image passes along to yet another part of the brain, the inferior temporal cortex, which contains specialized neurons that recognize form, depth and color. It is like having several transparent maps—one showing streets, another general topographic features, another the colors of the ground—and you lay them down one atop the other until you perceive enough detail to tell where you are.

Object recognition is even further specialized. This part of your brain is highly skilled at recognizing people's faces, with specific neurons dedicated to this important task. This ability explains why you can remember someone's face long after you have forgotten his or her name, or even where you met. Which also explains why we so often ask the question: "Don't I know you from somewhere?"

The visual system is a marvelous example of what the brain does so well—it breaks sensory inputs apart into separate, manageable components and then reassembles them in customized ways to achieve a particular goal. Hearing is another example of this extraordinary ability. No audio technology equals our auditory system's sensitivity to sound. We can detect sounds ranging from 20 to 20,000 Hertz, with a million-fold range in loudness. Because your brain receives its inputs in stereo, by comparing differences in input from your ears, you can locate a sound precisely in space. With stereo hearing, you can cross a room in total darkness and touch the speaker of a radio or the top of the head of someone speaking softly, assuming you don't stumble over the sofa.

The neurons in your inner ear, called hair cells, are like tiny amplifiers tuned to respond to a specific frequency. Frequency signals are then carried to precise locations in the temporal lobes, which are along the sides of the brain. In much the same way that your visual system works, outputs are projected onto different sound maps within your brain, which then reassembles a jigsaw puzzle of frequencies into something we can understand—music, speech or car horns. One part of the temporal lobe, called the medial superior nucleus, compares differences in sound to locate its source. Another specialized function, one that is particularly well-developed among musicians, is perfect pitch (see sidebar).

Taste and touch operate in a similar manner. Inputs from the senso-

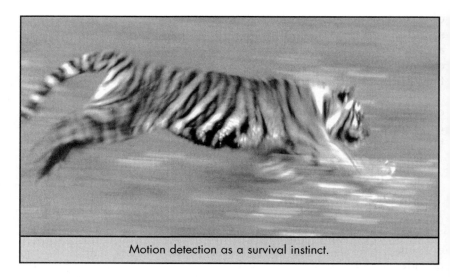

Motion detection as a survival instinct.

ry neurons are transmitted to specialized locations in the brain. For touch, the area is a broad stripe of cortex in the middle of the brain, running from the top almost to the bottom. Toe sensations are mapped at the top, followed in descending order by the knees, legs, torso, shoulders, fingers, neck, head and face. Your body recognizes the sense of touch in your fingers and face as being of prime importance, and devotes extraordinarily large amounts of the cortex to processing inputs from these areas.

The sensory part of your brain is all about breaking down environmental stimuli into manageable bits and presenting sensory inputs in a coherent manner to your conscious mind. Your mind then picks and chooses what it wants to pay the most attention to. When the brain has trouble reassembling the broken images of the outside world, mental illness can result. This appears to be especially true in schizophrenia.

The Making of Memories

Learning and memory are perhaps the most critical of our brain functions. Most of what we do—driving a car, cooking a meal, taking out the trash—must be learned. It involves, in the case of driving, a mix of incoming data about road conditions ("The road looks icy.") and stored knowledge ("I know there's a bend up ahead.") to produce an appropriate response ("Apply brakes gently!"). Learning is the process of acquiring new information, while memory is the process of retaining that information in a form that can be accessed later.

Memory is a remarkably handy and hardy device. Picture life without a reliable memory. Leaving your home each day, you would need a large sign: LOCK DOOR UPON EXITING. In fine print, the sign would then provide detailed instructions:

1) Locate door key—a flat metallic object with grooves on one side that generally resides in your pocket.

2) Insert key into the cylinder on the front of the door.

3) Turn to the right, then return to vertical.

4) Withdraw key from cylinder and return it to pocket.

Naturally, this example presupposes you have a memory for words and language and that you remember what the words pants, metal, cylinder and vertical mean. But with a properly operating memory, you can quickly depart your house without resorting to complex instructions at each step. You can start your car, back out of the driveway and drive to work or school.

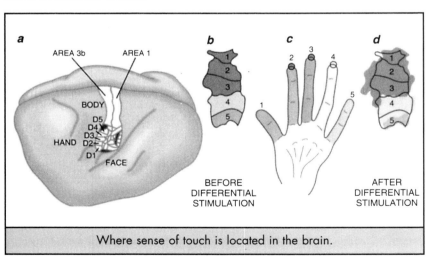

a

AREA 3b   AREA 1

BODY
D5
D4
D3
HAND D2
D1
FACE

b

c

d

BEFORE
DIFFERENTIAL
STIMULATION

AFTER
DIFFERENTIAL
STIMULATION

Where sense of touch is located in the brain.

Memory's Grand Central Station

Just as language, motion and vision have their own distinct areas of the brain, so does memory. Back in the 1950s, neurosurgeons at the Montreal Neurological Institute inadvertently discovered the part of the brain where memories are stored.

One unfortunate patient of the Montreal institute was a 27-year-old assembly-line worker identified only as "H.M." who had severe epilepsy. After surgery in 1953 that removed portions of the temporal lobes on both sides of his head, he had fewer seizures, but he now suffered from a devastating memory problem. He could no longer store long-term memories. He could still remember the people, events and places he had experienced before surgery and he had a normal I.Q. What he couldn't do was translate short-term memory into long-term. For instance, a doctor might enter H.M.'s room, introduce herself, hold a conversation with him and then leave. If she then returned a few minutes later, H.M. could remember neither her name, her face, nor even the fact that a doctor had ever come to visit him. It turned out that H.M.'s doctors had removed the very part of the brain, now known as the hippocampus, which is essential to forming lasting memories.

It was thought that without his hippocampus H.M. could learn nothing new, that he was forever stuck in the mental present. In an interview he describe his plight. "Right now, I'm wondering, have I done or said anything amiss. You see, at this moment everything looks clear to me, but what happened just before? That's what worries me. It's like waking from a dream. I just don't remember."

However, as H.M. later demonstrated, the brain has many types of memory. He could learn a repetitive motion task, like serving a tennis ball, and with practice, he would get better and better, day after day. But imagine being H.M.'s tennis instructor. On day five of practice, say, you would have to introduce yourself for the fifth time, and then you might once again teach him how to serve the ball. But if you congratulate H.M. on the improvement in his service, he would probably say: "Improvement? What are you talking about, this is the first time I've ever played tennis."

The example of H.M. clearly demonstrates that there are many types of memory. Movement, sound, smell, taste and vision all are

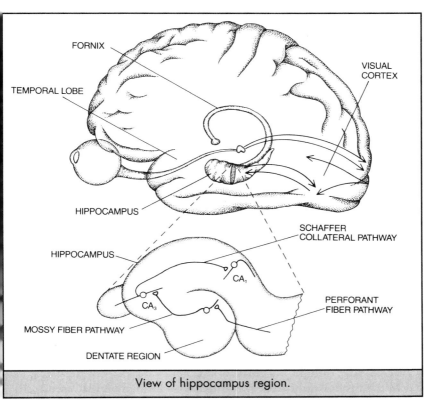

FORNIX

VISUAL CORTEX

TEMPORAL LOBE

HIPPOCAMPUS

SCHAFFER COLLATERAL PATHWAY

HIPPOCAMPUS

CA₁

PERFORANT FIBER PATHWAY

CA₃

MOSSY FIBER PATHWAY

DENTATE REGION

View of hippocampus region.

located in separate places in the brain, and each has its own memory depository. It turns out that when it comes to practiced motion, there is a kind of learning that takes place right in the area of the brain that controls that movement. Remembered movement can be termed "procedural" memory because such learning does not require the conscious attention needed to remember facts, figures, words, names and such; that process is known as "declarative" memory. And as will be seen below, practice makes perfect by increasing the amount of neural matter devoted to an area. Memory, which takes many forms and resides in many locations, is just another example of the parallel-distributed processing of most brain functions.

The prefrontal lobes appear to have multiple temporary-memory areas, each one devoted to different tasks such as the locations of objects; the size, color and shape of objects; words and sounds; or mathematical operations. The ultimate function of working memory is to stimulate or suppress activity in other regions of the brain. For instance, you see a yellow light, make the connection between a yellow light and the impending need to stop, and then send a signal to the motor cortex, which in turn coordinates the request for action and sends a signal to the right foot to either stomp on the brake or on the accelerator, depending on your inclination.

One of the most important chemicals involved in the working memory is the neurotransmitter dopamine. An imbalance in the levels of dopamine in the prefrontal cortex can be seriously debilitating. For example, scientists have found that the brains of old monkeys can become deficient in this neurotransmitter; as a result, they have a hard time with tests that require working memory. Injecting these elderly simians with dopamine, though, restores their working memory.

Research into how the working memory and frontal lobes work under normal conditions also gives clues to what goes wrong when memory fails. Neuroscientists have implicated the prefrontal cortex in many psychiatric and neurological conditions, especially schizophrenia. The abnormal mental states seen in schizophrenia look very much like those caused by physical damage to the prefrontal lobes—thought disorders, limited attention span, inappropriate emotional responses and lack of future goals and direction. Without a properly functioning prefrontal cortex, scientists say, you cannot bring the various components of thought and response together.

Language and Thought

Language is a unique trait of human beings, but it did not fall from the sky and land upon our species fully formed. Language evolved. Humans, and the species that preceded them in the evolutionary chain, had to first develop the ability to categorize and efficiently store away actions and mental images of objects, events and the relationships between them. Language arose in the process of evolution because it is such an efficient vehicle for compressing all this information into man-

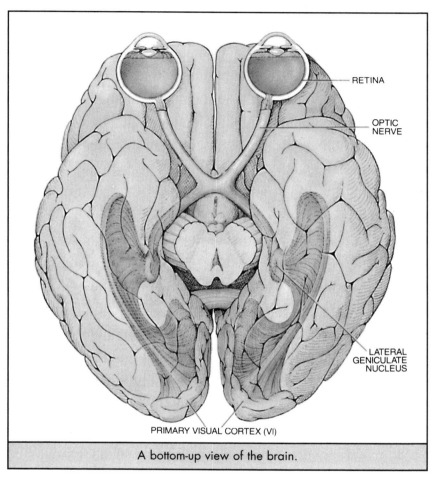

RETINA

OPTIC NERVE

LATERAL GENICULATE NUCLEUS

PRIMARY VISUAL CORTEX (VI)

A bottom-up view of the brain.

ageable bits. Saying the word "computer," for instance, can evoke several images: lap-top computer, desk-top computer, robots, computer that took over the world, etc.

Language evolved not only as an efficient means of communication, but also as an indispensable tool for thinking. Much of what we call thought is represented as a string of words, with the occasional image

A Perfectly Pitched Mind

Mozart.

Scientists in Germany believe they have discovered an enlarged part of the brain which may have contributed to the enormous talent of such musical geniuses as Ludwig von Beethoven and Wolfgang Amadeus Mozart. What many talented musicians have is an attribute called perfect pitch, the ability to distinguish a musical note heard in isolation as easily as most people can distinguish one word from the next.

The German scientists used a brain-scanning technique called positron emission tomography (PET). Not all musicians have perfect pitch, of course, but with PET scans the researchers found that those who possess the attribute have an enlarged left planum temporale, a structure on the temporal lobe that is involved in speech, among other things. Musicians without perfect pitch, as well as non-musicians, had smaller planum temporales than the gifted musicians.

Early exposure to music is important in developing perfect pitch. Those with perfect pitch began their musical training before the age of seven. If a child is exposed to music after age 10, it appears the brain no longer has the plasticity to rewire its neurons into a pattern that accommodates perfect pitch. Apparently, the creation of musical genius requires a combination of nature and nurture.

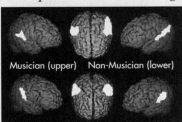

Musician (upper)   Non-Musician (lower)

or sensation thrown in. We can switch effortlessly between silent interior thinking to thinking out loud. For instance, you might be shuffling around the house muttering,"Now where did I put my wallet." Another family member might say, "Huh?" To which you grumpily reply, "Oh nothing, just thinking out loud."

Whether it be read, written, heard or spoken, language is another example of how the brain coordinates the activities of scattered pockets of neurons. Brain-imaging studies have shown that the areas of the brain that are activated vary depending on what the action is. While hearing words, areas of the temporal lobe associated with reception of sound are the most active. When reading words, it is the occipital lobes associated with vision that come into play. To speak words, activity jumps up to the motor areas along the upper middle of the brain. But to actually generate the words we speak, brain activity increases dramatically in the frontal lobes, where the previously mentioned mental blackboard is found. If the connections between these areas are disrupted through either damage or a disturbance in the body's biochemistry, there will be trouble. A person might be able to think about words, but if the connections to the area involved in actually speaking them are disturbed, those words will never come out. This disruption is commonly seen in stroke victims.

Thought, then, is simply the most elegant form of the same complex parallel-distributed processing that happens in most of the brain's activity. Thought, and the language it gives rise to, are powerful systems of representing and interacting with the world. They have allowed us to create civilizations, to develop music and dance and culture, and to devise means of passing our knowledge on to the next generation through teaching and written records. But this power comes at a price. When essential links in the train of mental activity break down or are destroyed, then the elegant system becomes disordered. We can become depressed or psychotic, hear voices where there are none, see things that do not exist, become forgetful or frightened, and generally come to live a miserable existence.

The issue of how best to heal a troubled mind will be discussed in the chapters ahead. For the neuroscientist, the answer is drugs or surgery, and for the psychologist the answer is talk therapy. Each approach has had its triumphs and failures, as we shall see.

CHAPTER SIX

The Major
Mental Illnesses

or thousands of years, poets and priests have seen madness as an affliction of the soul. On the other side, medical practitioners, at least since the days of Hippocrates, have viewed it as a brain disease, but one touched off by an imbalance in the humors, or by the wanderings of the uterus. It has only been in the twentieth century that we have really been able to peer down into the depths of the brain and determine the aberrations in its structure and biochemical functioning, and by doing so begin to construct a biological view of what today we call mental illness. As we've seen in the preceding chapters, the neuroscientists of today look at the brain as a complex parallel-distributed processing organ that can at times fall into disarray. Below we examine some of the findings that have emerged from their quest for a scientific explanation for madness.

Schizophrenia: Breaking with the World

Schizophrenia is pretty well misunderstood by most people. The disease is not about the presence of more than one personality in the same mind, an affliction known as multiple-personality disorder. Instead, schizophrenia involves the fragmentation of the internal thought process. The parallel-distributed processing system breaks down so that people with schizophrenia have difficulty putting reality together. What they have is not a split personality; rather, the split is with the rest of the world, with the reality outside.

Schizophrenia has been portrayed as a romantic illness, a sort of brilliant madness, or as an alternate but valid way of viewing reality. But the chaotic jumble of thoughts and sensations is devastating for sufferers. Vincent van Gogh was a man capable of creating stunning works of art, but many of his paintings seem to reflect the altered view of reality he experienced, leading some psychia-

Depression.

trists to conclude that he was afflicted with schizophrenia. Others contend that van Gogh's disease was bipolar disorder (manic-depression). Whichever mental illness it was, he found it crippling, not liberating. He painted for only 10 years of his life, ultimately resorting to the only effective treatment that would end his suffering—suicide. He profoundly regretted having mental illness. "As for me, you must know that I shouldn't precisely have chosen madness if there had been a choice," he wrote to his brother Theo. "Oh, if I could have worked without this accursed disease—what things I might have done."

Schizophrenia hits about one percent of the population, wherever they are in the world. Unlike depression, from which people will often completely recover, schizophrenia usually lasts a lifetime and worsens with time. Only about 25 percent of those diagnosed with the disease will be "cured," and it appears that this first group will recover whether or not they are given antipsychotic drugs. The next 25 percent respond well to medication and get along pretty well as long as they continue taking antipsychotics. They can live independently, marry and even hold down a job. The remaining 50 percent of schizophrenics end up more or less permanently disabled, showing little or no improvement. They spend their days in nursing homes, halfway houses, psychiatric hospitals and prisons, or out on the streets. About 10 percent of all people afflicted with schizophrenia will be dead within 10 years of being first diagnosed, sometimes from violent encounters with others, but often from suicide.

People with schizophrenia will occasionally commit crimes during a psychotic episode. For instance, John Hinckley, Jr. shot President Reagan because his disordered thinking led him to believe that this act

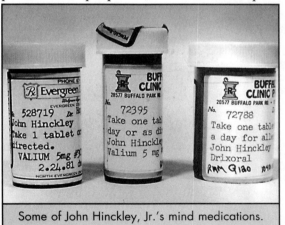

Some of John Hinckley, Jr.'s mind medications.

Van Gogh's "Wheatfield with Cypress."

would earn him the love of actress Jodie Foster. This is quite a different thing from, say, a man who quite rationally plots to kill his wife in order to collect on her insurance policy. Actually, the potential of schizophrenia sufferers to commit violent acts tends to be overblown in the media; a person with antisocial personality disorder is more likely to commit a violent crime (see below).

To be diagnosed with schizophrenia, a person has to be ill for six months with at least one psychotic phase, and during psychosis there must be:

1) Bizarre delusions, such as being controlled by a chip implanted by the CIA.
2) Hallucinations, usually hearing voices.
3) Disordered thoughts and possibly a loss of emotion in a person's speech and actions.

Schizophrenia rendered artistically by Louise Williams.

A person with schizophrenia has tremendous difficulty sorting out, interpreting and then properly responding to the sensory inputs coming in from the surrounding world. As one schizophrenic patient put it: "When people are talking I have to think what the words mean. You see, there is an interval instead of a spontaneous response." As another has said: "Everything is in bits. You put the picture up bit by bit in your head. It's like a photograph that's torn in bits and put together again. If you move it's frightening."

So what causes this breakdown in reality? It now appears that schizophrenia is primarily a brain disorder, and does not result from being reared in a dysfunctional family, as some psychiatrists earlier theorized. It is also quite possible that the disease has a strong genetic component. While the incidence of schizophrenia is one percent in the general populace, it rises sharply to 15 percent in the parents, children and siblings of those who suffer from the disease. And the chance that the identical twin of a person with schizophrenia will also be stricken is a frightening 48 percent. What's really interesting about this statistic, though, is that 52 percent of identical twins don't come down with schizophrenia when their genetically identical siblings are afflicted, which indicates that there's more at work in this disease than just genes. There must also be an environmental component of some sort at work, such as brain injury or infection, that touches off the disease.

Many areas of the brain are thought to be affected in schizophrenia. There seems to be some as-yet-unexplained imbalance in the way nerve impulses are transmitted at the synapses or how they are processed by collections of neurons in distinct parts of the brain. Some scientific research suggests the prefrontal lobes are involved, while other evidence points to the temporal lobes, but it is still not clear precisely what the defect is or where it is located.

Negotiating the Highs and Lows of Bipolar Disorder and Depression

Bipolar disorder, formerly known as manic-depressive illness, strikes about one-half of one percent to one percent of the population. Bipolar disorder, as its name implies, induces euphoric highs that impart tremendous mental and physical energy, not unlike the high

Bipolar sufferer Edgar Allen Poe.

that drugs and alcohol produce. While in the grip of mania, people with the disorder can feel on top of the world, in love with life. They're often as fast-talking and quick-witted as Robin Williams, but they're on this high all the time, not just while on camera. This natural high sounds terrific, so what's the problem?

The euphoria of bipolar disorder can last for weeks. And people in this manic state of mind do some pretty wild and foolish things. Schizophrenics are usually too disordered to act on their impulses, while depressives are too lethargic to act on their distorted thinking, but manics are delusional but also full of energy.

One University of California student called the Kremlin to try to talk the Soviet leader into banning the bomb. He didn't get through to Brezhnev himself but he did talk at length to a member of the Politburo. Sounds harmless enough, but he ran up an $850 phone bill during this escapade, which his parents were obliged to pay, and the bomb was not banned as a result of his well-intentioned but impractical efforts.

Mania can be hurtful and destructive for the family of the afflicted individual, who have to pick up the pieces in the wake of this mental tornado. Psychiatrist Ronald Fieve, in his book *Moodswing*, described the actions of one of his patients during a manic episode:

"All by himself, he had been building a magnificent swimming pool for his country home in Virginia, working 18 hours a day at it. He decided to make the pool public and open [a] concession stand at one end to help defray the mounting costs of the project. When his wife suggested that he might be going overboard, he became furious and threatened to leave her for another woman . . . Complaining that his wife was a stick-in-the-mud, he decided to throw a round-the-clock party, and he invited to the house almost everyone he passed on the street." Not everyone with bipolar disorder goes off the deep end with their impractical schemes. Some are able to channel their mania into heightened productivity, or at least wait it out. Many famous creative people have been afflicted, such as the poets Anne Sexton and Walt Whitman, authors Ernest Hemingway and Edgar Allen Poe, and world leaders like Winston Churchill.

Major Depression

Major depression is one of the most common mental illnesses. At some point, about 20 percent of women and about 10 percent of men will have what would be defined as a major depression. In the past, depression was thought to result from psychological dysfunction; that is, depression is caused by personal problems. Today's thinking, though, is that personal problems are actually the result of depression's deleterious effects on mood and on the ability to work and to interact properly with others.

Untreated with drugs, major depressions can last six to nine months. About half of the people who have one major depression will never have another, but those who do have a second episode will usually have three or more bouts. Sometimes they erupt for no apparent reason, or they can be

Bipolar disorder drove Ernest Hemingway to suicide.

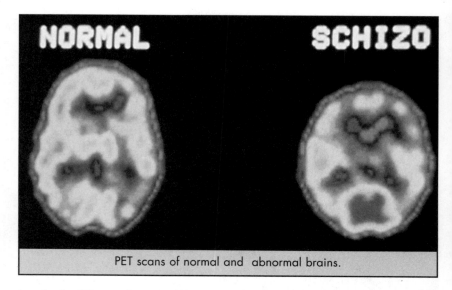
PET scans of normal and abnormal brains.

touched off by such major life events as the diagnosis of cancer, a death in the family or a criminal conviction. Like bipolar disorder, major depression is a life-threatening illness, with 15 percent of those afflicted eventually committing suicide, a rate 25 times greater than that of the general population.

With major depression there is often profound sadness that is paralyzing and unrelenting. It starts in the morning and lasts all day; it wakes people up at night, or keeps them in bed until noon. Depression can take another, more subtle, form. It can make a person lose interest in life. A hockey fan might skip the playoffs, interest in a formerly active sex life might evaporate or a father might stop playing with the kids.

A quarter of those suffering from major depression will also hallucinate, a symptom one might associate more with schizophrenia. They may hear voices, see dead relatives or demons, or smell foul odors. When they hear these voices, the soundtrack is not like a schizoid delusion which might say something like: "The C.I.A. is controlling your mind with a microchip." Instead, the voices reflect the depressed mood, and sound more like: "You are vile, fat and disgusting."

Both major depression and bipolar disorder seem to run in families.

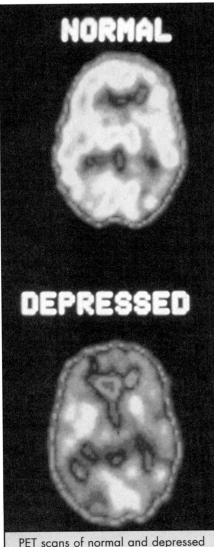

NORMAL

DEPRESSED

PET scans of normal and depressed brains.

For example, if one identical twin becomes profoundly depressed, the other has a 78 percent chance of also developing the disease, a rate higher than the incidence of schizophrenia among identical twins. Despite this observation and vigorous efforts by geneticists, no one has yet found the precise gene or genes that account for the disease, although renewed efforts are underway to find the bipolar genes. Lacking a genetic explanation, some researchers believe that these diseases are not genetic, but might be caused instead by environmental factors—by a brain infection, a head injury, or simply by a buildup of life's stresses.

Actually, stress does seem to play a big role in touching off major depression. Studies show that the rate of depression has been rising dramatically in the twentieth century, not only in the U.S., but throughout the world. In Italy, for instance, eight percent of the population born between 1905 and 1914 developed depression by the time they reached age 30, but for those born between 1945 and 1955, the rate jumped to 18 percent.

Researchers suspect that the increase in depression is a side effect of the late-twentieth-centu-

Winston Churchill.

ry lifestyle. The nuclear family has eroded; most people don't grow up knowing or living near their extended family; parents don't spend as much time with their children. All these stresses add up to a greater susceptibility to depression. It seems to be a combination disease, in which stress plus susceptibility equals depression.

Despite our knowing little about what actually causes these disorders on a neurochemical level, the fact remains that antidepressant drugs work. Another undisputed fact is that psychotherapy, in particular cognitive therapy (see chapter 7), is also effective—by itself or in combination with drugs—to snap people out of what Winston Churchill called the "black dog" of depression.

Anxiety and Compulsion

Up until now, we have been talking about disorders of mood and of thought. These are devastating illnesses, but what psychiatrists actually see most are the ones that involve fear of some sort. These anxiety states go by names like post traumatic stress disorder, panic attacks, and obsessive-compulsive disorder; all of them involve some form of fear and dread that is out of proportion with reality. For example, it's normal for a soldier to be terrified on the battlefield, but it's not normal for him to have a panic attack ten years later while driving to a shopping mall.

Phobias

The most common anxiety disorders are phobias, which take the form of a fear of heights (acrophobia), confined spaces (claustrophobia), spiders (arachnophobia), flying, public speaking and so on. All of us have aversions of some sort, but they do not warrant the label "phobia" until they overwhelm a person with anxiety or completely prevent them from carrying out the necessary activities of life. About 10 percent of the population has a significant phobia, but many anxious people can get by without treatment simply by avoiding heights, or airplanes, or making speeches, or whatever situation bedevils them. Obviously, avoidance can take a toll in a person's professional life and treatment is considered the preferred route to dealing with serious phobias.

Panic Attacks

Panic attacks are brief but intense recurrent episodes of terror that seem to spring from nowhere without cause or warning. They are not associated with situations that would normally be expected to elicit fearful responses, or with situations where a person is the focus of attention, and may suffer stage fright.

The attacks only last 15–30 minutes, but the terror they induce activates the sympathetic nervous system which in turn releases hormones that cause a frantic heart beat, profuse sweating and trembling. The symptoms can be so intense that people in the throes of a panic attack often think they are about to die and will take themselves to an emergency room. Panic attacks can also be associated with agoraphobia, the fear of public places, which is where these attacks often take place. In her book *The Broken Brain*, Nancy Andreasen describes Greg, a 27-year-old computer programmer. One day while driving on the bridge he had to cross every day to get to work, he was seized by an image of what would happen should his tiny foreign car be involved in an accident. He pictured it crumpled like a beer can, with him inside dying a bloody and lingering death. Even worse, he imagined his car falling from the bridge in an accident, and himself drowning in the river below.

During this first panic attack his heart was racing, his breath came in gasps and he had to pull over to try to regain composure. He started having these bridge-crossing panic attacks more and more frequently and began calling in sick so much—to avoid the crossing—that his employer ordered him into psychiatric therapy. By that time, he was essentially housebound because he was even having the attacks driving to a nearby shopping mall.

People who suffer from these bouts of terror seem to have a very different neurochemistry than those who don't. For instance, panic-attacks can be induced in people who are prone to them by injecting them with sodium lactate or by having them inhale carbon monoxide, both of which cause a sudden drop in the pH of their blood, as happens when a person

Lady Macbeth.

hyperventilates. People with normal brain function are not sensitive to these substances; neither are panic-attack sufferers who take antidepressant drugs.

The limbic system, which is thought to play a big role in the expression of emotion, seems to be involved in touching off panic attacks, and neuroscientists think they have pinpointed the part responsible for these attacks—the right parahippocampal gyrus. This area seems to be the panic center for the brain, in both normal people and panic-attack sufferers. Using PET scans of the brains of people prone to panic attacks, researchers found that this area of the limbic system has an excessive blood flow, meaning it is drawing too much oxygen and consuming far more sugar than is normal. It turns out this overactivity in the right parahippocampal gyrus is going on whether a person is in the middle of a panic attack or not. It's as if the panic center has a hair trigger. Anti-anxiety drugs help calm down the overactive panic center.

Obsessive-Compulsive Disorder

In obsessive-compulsive disorder (OCD), people have recurrent thoughts that are hard to switch off, a grimmer version of that catchy tune that you can't stop humming. Obsessive thoughts are intrusive and senseless visual images, ideas or impulses that often involve violence or contamination. Compulsions are repetitive behaviors that are performed in a ritualistic manner, in response to the obsessive thoughts. The problem for people afflicted with OCD is that their nonstop thoughts compel them to engage in behaviors that interfere with work, friendships and family life.

Shakespeare portrayed obsessive-compulsive behavior quite well in his character Lady Macbeth, who is filled with dread and anxiety over her role in the murder of King Duncan. She is obsessed with the thought that her hands are still stained with the blood of the dead king, although it has in fact been washed away. "Out, damned spot," she shrieks as she rubs and rubs at the nonexistent blood. As one character in the play observes: "It is an accustomed action of her, to seem thus washing her hands: I have known her continue in this a quarter of an hour."

Another obsession might be the thought that one has hit someone while driving, even though nothing was actually felt or seen. In response to this thought, the affected person might have an irresistible compulsion to turn the car around and search the "scene of the crime" for a body. And they may have to repeat the search three or four times until the obsession is finally relieved. Satisfying a compulsion can cause the sufferer to miss an exam, or work, or other important appointments.

What causes obsessive-compulsive disorder? Freud said it was a classic example of how guilt and repression act on the subconscious to produce bizarre inexplicable physical symptoms. But even Freud found OCD to be especially resistant to psychoanalysis.

There is some scientific evidence that OCD is a genetic defect. One theory is that it may be an alternative form of Tourette's disorder, which afflicts about one person in every 2,000. People with Tourette's have "tics," that compel them to nod, shuffle, hop, stick out the tongue, and to shout and mumble obscene words. In the family of a Tourette's sufferer, there will often be others with OCD. In other words, OCD may be a milder version of Tourette's. The biological explanation for OCD is further supported by the fact that the condition isn't easily treated with psychotherapy and that antidepressant drugs like Prozac and Luvox can control the disorder. So it appears that OCD may be yet another neurochemical imbalance in the brain.

Post Traumatic Stress Disorder

Post traumatic stress disorder (PTSD) has been described as a natural reaction to an unnatural life event. Post traumatic stress disorder has been around for a long time, of course, but it wasn't until thousands of Vietnam veterans were found to have it that it began to be taken seri-

The psychic trauma of combat lives on after war's end.

ously. A combat veteran may have had to kill a person at close range, or may have killed civilians intentionally or inadvertently, or might have seen a close friend blown to bits. Other traumatic situations may touch off PTSD. A firefighter may fail to find all the trapped victims in a fire, or an emergency medical technician might arrive on the scene of a horrendous air crash, or a woman might be raped and brutalized. All of these events can lodge themselves in the mind and cause symptoms of PTSD.

The Vietnam veteran might wake up suddenly from sleep and dive for cover, or leap off a bicycle while riding through terrain reminiscent of the scene of combat. The stress may build to the point that friends or family become the targets of outbursts of explosive temper, or the sufferer may resort to heavy drug use.

Because PTSD is such a concrete anxiety disorder touched off by very tangible events—as opposed to OCD with its more mysterious and possibly biological origins—it is usually amenable to treatment with antianxiety drugs and psychotherapy of a type that allows the venting of pent-up rage and fear. What has baffled some researchers is that many people who experience intense combat or other equally stressful traumas never develop PTSD. They apparently have PTSD-resistant personalities.

Personality Disorders

Everyone has personality traits. They are the patterns that determine how we see and think about our environment and how we relate to ourselves and others. These traits become disorders when they are inflexible and cause serious social or personal problems. For example, we all feel suspicious at times, but when someone is suspicious all the time about everyone they meet, they have what is called a paranoid personality disorder. In the avoidant personality disorder, the sufferer is not agoraphobic as a result of panic attacks. Instead, they have such low self-esteem and are so fearful of rejection that they become reclusive.

People with dependent personality disorder also have low self-esteem. They are fearful or incapable of making decisions, which they end up turning over to others. A woman with dependent personality disorder, for example, will put up with her husband's affairs or drunkenness or even physical abuse for fear that if she protests he will leave

Aftermath of violence: motorcycle-gang shootout.

her for good. In the borderline personality disorder, the sufferer is unstable and unpredictable—reclusive, quiet and calm one week, and the next gambling, partying, overdosing on drugs or running up big bills as a way of cutting loose.

People with personality disorders may cause their friends and family great distress, but they generally only harm themselves, not others. But the antisocial personality disorder is quite different. Someone with this disorder is indifferent to the feelings and rights of others, and may wear labels like "sick," "twisted" or "psycho." It is fairly common, affecting about one percent of females and three percent of males in their teens and twenties. And it appears that it plays a role in drug abuse and criminal or sadistic behavior. But the psychiatric community is divided on how to regard the antisocial personality. Not all violent criminals are actually afflicted with this disorder. Some are just plain mean; others want to take revenge on others for a perceived hurt; still others are lazy and would rather rob than work. Psychiatrists, and the rest of society, are uncertain how to identify those with antisocial personality disorder, or whether to even try. Some say they are all criminals, not "victims" of some "disorder," and should be locked up. Others argue that the mentally ill should be segregated from the general criminal population and given psychotherapy. The debate is far from over, but the public, at least, seems to be leaning very definitely toward simply locking criminals up, and dispensing with the psychotherapy.

People with antisocial personality disorder show such traits as a history of illegal or malicious activities starting before age 15 and continuing into adulthood; instability and irresponsibility in dealing with work, friendships and parenthood; recklessness and aggressiveness, often resulting in fights; and constant lying.

What causes such personality disorders? Behavioral psychologists contend that their roots can be traced to traumatic events in childhood. In the case of antisocial behavior, the event might be sexual or physical abuse, or the absence of strong parental figures plus immersion in a violent, drug-laced culture. The problem is that individual psychotherapy has not proven to be particularly effective with such people. What does seem to work, however, is to intervene early and aggressively, involving both parents and child in family therapy, in which parents are taught to better monitor their child's behavior and apply more consistent corrective actions.

Some scientists strongly believe that much antisocial and violent behavior is governed by genes and that tests will soon be developed that can detect those with a high likelihood of committing violent crimes. "With the expected advances, we're going to be able to diagnose many people who are biologically brain-prone to violence," claims Stuart Yudofsky, chairman of the psychiatry department at the Baylor College of Medicine in Houston. He contends that America should replace its punishment-based approach to justice with a medical model which emphasizes diagnosis, prevention and treatment before antisocial behavior erupts.

Brain-imaging studies have shown that the brains of violent criminals often show less activity in their frontal lobes than those of nonviolent people. In one study of murderers, about 75 percent seemed to have low metabolic activity in the frontal lobes, which is the area thought to regulate aggression. Other studies show that low levels of serotonin seem to be linked to impulsive and aggressive behavior. But some researchers doubt that the solution to crime is to give every child inclined toward violence antidepressant drugs. They say that aggressive and violent behaviors are normal responses to a threatening world. Better to change that world than to hand out drugs to everyone in it.

Attention Deficit Disorder

Every elementary school seems to have a few children who just can't keep still, finish their work or focus their attention for more than a few minutes. Such children interrupt, butt into games, and blow up in frustration if made to wait their turn. These kids often are diagnosed as having attention deficit hyperactivity disorder (ADHD, or ADD), which is the most common reason children are brought to therapy. It is said to afflict from two percent to five percent of the school-age population, but some psychologists say it's an overused label that is too often slapped on kids who are simply "hard to control."

Brain scans show that people with ADD have less than normal metabolic activity in the parts of their brain associated with focusing attention, which is why hyperactive children are given stimulants like Ritalin instead of tranquilizers. Picture the attention-focusing parts of the brain as the mind's rudder. A ship with a broken rudder is buffeted about by the winds. To regain control, the solution is to fix the rudder, not take down the sails. Ritalin fixes the brain's rudder by stimulating the attention-focusing structures of the brain, allowing a child's natural talents to emerge.

Psychotherapy can also be of benefit to kids and even adults with ADD by helping them like and accept themselves despite having the disorder. It can also help them overcome the anxiety and depression that accompanies a negative self-image. In psychotherapy, they talk about their upsetting thoughts and feelings and identify self-defeating patterns of behavior. The therapist will help them explore ways to change.

Identical twins Joseph and Tommy Williams, killers of David Powell.

Creativity and Mental Illness

"Why is it that all men who are outstanding in philosophy, poetry or the arts are melancholic?" asked Aristotle back in the fourth century B.C. Today the answer is coming from new research that indicates a link between genius and madness. Psychiatrists have found that among famous artists, the rates of depression and bipolar disorder are from 10 to 30 times greater than they are in the wider population. Another study found the rate of alcoholism is 60 percent in actors and 41 percent in novelists, but the rate drops to just 10 percent among military officers, who are often portrayed as a hard-drinking bunch. The rate drops even further, down to just three percent, among scientists such as engineers and astrophysicists.

The highs and lows of depression and bipolar disorder seem to force people to face a much wider range of emotional experience. In surviving the hardship of their illness, it appears they are left with a richer palette of experience than non-afflicted people, according to Ruth Richards, psychiatrist and author of *Creativity and the Healthy Mind*. Other psychiatrists contend that the eruption of energy seen in a manic episode, for instance, may give rise to a flood of ideas the mind can later sort through and shape into something useful during times of depression or normality.

In the case of the composer Robert Schumann, his bouts of mania were not necessarily debilitating but his depressions ultimately proved fatal. Schumann apparently entered into extended periods of hypomania, a less extreme form of the usual mania seen in bipolar disorder, and this hypomania seems to result in original thinking, according to psychiatrist Kay Redfield Jamison, author of *Touched with Fire*: *Manic-Depressive Illness and the Artistic Temperament*.

Schumann wrote 24 musical compositions in 1840—as many as he had in all of the eight previous years—and Jamison says this was because he was hypomanic throughout that year. His productivity plunged in subsequent years, until in 1844 he produced no musical compositions and attempted suicide. Schumann gradually recovered his creativity, so much so that during another yearlong bout of hypomania in 1849 he produced a record 27 scores. He apparently collapsed into depression again, so that by 1854 he was producing nothing and again attempted suicide. By 1856, Schumann was dead, having starved himself to death in an insane asylum.

With powerful drugs in their arsenal, psychiatrists face a dilemma when dealing with the artistically gifted. Leaving the disease untreated may result in suicide, but treatment often blunts creativity. As Jamison writes, "Left untreated, however, manic-depressive illness often worsens over time—and no one is creative when severely depressed, psychotic or dead. The bouts of mania and depression grow more and more frequent and more severe."

Her hope is that new drugs will come along that can control bipolar disorder without dampening creativity.

The Psychotherapies

N o discussion of mind medicines is complete without a look at psychotherapy. Today's psychotherapy is quite different from the psychoanalysis pioneered by Sigmund Freud, which often involved almost daily sessions that went on for months and sometimes years. Quite a bit has changed in terms of technique since Freud's original psychoanalysis. There have been many branchings from those roots, with an explosion in the 1960s and 1970s of new therapies designed to make people feel happier and more fulfilled. Today there are about 400 separate brands of psychotherapy in America. Many of these new therapies are untested and their efficacy is doubtful, but they have flourished in a climate in which someone else, typically an insurance company, was helping to pay the bill.

In the current political and economic climate of healthcare reform and cost-containment, however, the medical bill-payers—be they employers, insurance companies or the government—are insisting that mental-health professionals deliver the most value for the money. They are not as interested in seeing patients happy and fulfilled as they are in seeing them returned to a functional state of existence; that is, well enough to return to work. As a result of the pressure to demonstrate fast and low-cost results, short-term psychotherapy, often combined with drug therapy, is now emerging as the favored treatment. In fact, one prominent psychotherapist, Nicholas Cummings, has proposed a Patient Bill of Rights for his profession: "The patient has a right to relief from pain, anxiety, and depression in the shortest time possible and with the least intrusive intervention." Cummings says it is the obligation of psychotherapists to perfect their skills to the point that they can fulfill this credo.

A psychotherapist.

Psychoanalysis and Psychodynamic Therapy

A psychiatric interview.

Freud saw the brain as a hopelessly complicated organ that we could never hope to understand. He felt that an understanding of the workings of the mind, not the brain, was the way to build therapies. To Freud, the source of neurosis was anxiety associated with the struggle of the ego, or conscious mind, with the id, the subconscious part of the mind that is the realm of primitive instincts and desires (see discussion in chapter 8). In classical Freudian psychoanalysis, patients lie upon a couch and do not actually face the therapist. They spontaneously relate their thoughts and feelings in a process called free association. By carefully examining this tumble of thoughts, the therapist and the patient can then piece together a picture of the origins of anxieties and neuroses, often relating to childhood traumas.

Psychoanalysis as originally practiced by Freud has almost completely vanished. Patients can indeed achieve insight into their problems with psychoanalysis, but it usually takes a person who is already quite intelligent and aggressive and who has plenty of money and time to devote to the process. What Freud gave birth to, and other practitioners later modified, is now known as psychodynamic therapy. This form of talk therapy still involves delving into the psychic traumas of childhood; the main difference is that now the therapist is not a passive observer but takes an active role in drawing out the source of conflict between ego and id. Even this approach is controversial and appears to also be heading for oblivion. For one thing, it's hard to prove that it's really helping people, or whether the mental disorder vanishes on its own. Proponents of psychodynamic therapy concede that it is expensive and time-consuming, but maintain that it does work.

Psychodynamic therapy is not recommended for psychotic conditions such as schizophrenia or for people with antisocial or psychopathic tendencies. It is for people who have interpersonal problems such as trouble finding relationships that work. In other words, it is good for neurotic or anxiety conditions.

Cognitive-Behavioral Therapy

Cognitive-behavioral therapy does not attempt to develop insight into the origin of a behavior. It is actually a combination of two approaches, and for certain problems it appears to be one of the most effective forms of psychotherapy currently available. The cognitive component attempts to modify or eliminate thought patterns that may be contributing to a person's problem; the problem could be drug use or panic attacks or some other maladjustments. The theory behind cognitive therapy is that the way people think about themselves and the surrounding world determines how they act. A student who believes she is bad at math will go on to do poorly in math, for instance. Therapists work to change this counterproductive thinking pattern.

The behavioral aspect addresses just the problematic behavior; no attempt is made to find out the deep underlying causes of the actions. Instead of focusing on a person's feelings, behavioral therapy focuses on action and may, for instance, use relaxation techniques to counteract panic attacks, or desensitization to slowly help a phobic person face the thing they dread.

In dealing with panic attacks, for instance, a therapist might meet with a patient for one to three hours a week and will search for the thoughts and feelings that accompany the attacks. The theory is that people with panic disorder have distortions of thinking they are unaware of that touch off a cycle of fear. The idea is to teach the patient to recognize the thoughts and feelings early in the process. They are taught to counteract thoughts like "This terrible feeling is getting worse. I'm about to have a panic attack" with calming thoughts like "Oh, it's just those symptoms again—they will pass."

Cognitive therapy seems to work wonders on many cases of major and moderate depression. It is designed to

Certain criminals can be helped with psychotherapy.

Child therapy.

counteract the negative self-images that depressed patients carry. For people with depression who are able to focus on the therapy it seems to be about as effective as antidepressants in snapping them out of it. Cocaine abuse can also yield to cognitive-behavioral therapy. In this case, the cognitive aspect of therapy focuses on laying out the harsh personal consequences of continuing to abuse drugs and the behavioral part deals with identifying ways to avoid cocaine cravings. Some treatment programs combine this psychotherapy with the antidepressant drug desipramine, which is thought to reduce cravings for cocaine.

Generally speaking, though, the majority of addicts will eventually return to their life of drugs. The treatment programs that seem to have the highest success rates tend to be those with the harshest methods. In Singapore, for instance, law enforcement is strict. The drug treatment programs there are run like boot camps, a sort of variation on the cognitive-behavioral approach in which users are shown the futility of continuing to take drugs. After they leave the centers, they have their urine checked once a week for illicit drugs. If they test positive, it's right back to boot camp. Even with these harsh measures, Singapore only has a 50 percent success rate in permanently straightening out drug abusers, which is about the highest verified long-term success rate in the world.

Cognitive-behavioral therapy has been applied in the U.S. to drug-abusing prisoners, with positive but not overwhelming results. In a 1993 study, of those who underwent the therapy, about 37 percent wound up back in prison within five years, while 55 percent of those who didn't take part in therapy returned to prison. Clearly, therapy made a difference in some people's lives.

Supportive Therapy

Even with medication, schizophrenia and other mental illnesses are a big burden and many sufferers will need what is called supportive psychotherapy. This is the same sort of counseling that is helpful in dealing with any debilitating disease, such as multiple sclerosis, severe diabetes or cancer. Supportive therapy deals with the here and now, not the past. The therapist provides practical advice and reassurance, and helps correct incorrect thinking. For instance, if the patent is convinced the CIA has put a computer chip in his brain and is using it to control him, the therapist sympathizes with how frightening that thought must be, while firmly pointing out that this just not the truth. The therapist will also provide practical guidance on how to avoid the kind of stressful circumstances that can lead to a psychotic episode that sends patients back to the hospital.

Community-based mental-health care.

Art as therapy.

Too Many Drugs?

Psychotherapy can be helpful in treating patients with mental disorders, but lengthy therapies that attempt to develop insight into the origins of problems can be expensive. Because of this, the bill-payers are forcing therapists to use the briefest treatments possible. In today's world of healthcare cost-cutting, psychotherapy is in a state of decline, while biological psychiatry, which sees brain disorders as the source of almost all mental illness, is the rising star. An overly strong belief in the biological viewpoint is leading to an over-dependence on psychopharmaceuticals to cure all mental ills, according to some psychiatrists. These anti-drug psychiatrists believe the ascendancy of drug therapy over talk therapy is unfortunate and misguided and may be causing as much mental disease as it is curing.

The Electronic Therapist

The age of computerized psychotherapy is here, much to the dismay of some psychiatrists. Companies are finding they cannot afford to pay for long-term therapy for patients who seem to be worried but otherwise well. What some companies have turned to is a program they feel is a cost-effective way of treating emotionally troubled workers. According to psychiatrist Roger Gould, who created the psychotherapy program, in traditional face-to-face therapy sessions, patients tend to ramble quite a bit telling stories from their life, which feels good at the time but really does not help the course of therapy. By working with the computer before seeing a therapist, they can identify issues that a human therapist later will focus on. The program might present the question: "In which areas of your life do you feel the most stress?" Responses might include a son or daughter's drug abuse, a spouse's infidelity, crying jags or arguments with the boss.

Talking to a computer is different from talking to a human therapist, says Gould. Patients will more readily tell a computer about incest, abuse or embarrassing incidents from the past precisely because it is not human. There is no shame, you are simply pressing buttons. The same information would have to be drawn out over many sessions with a human therapist, making the computer a valuable and cost-effective cotherapist.

Mental Illness Meets
the Modern Era

The history of the mind begins with the spirit and the soul. Primitive societies have all included people believed to have mystic powers, who can bring rain or sunshine, predict success in war, make crops grow and cure the ill. Today, we refer to the ones with these mystic powers as witches, wizards, priests or shamans. In every civilization, among Arabs, Chinese, Hebrews, Hindus and Greeks, the belief persisted that some form of possession by demons or vengeful spirits was the cause of madness. The ancient Babylonians had a rich spiritual world, inhabited by hordes of evil demons who battled those gods and spirits who were good. Of special concern was Idta, who caused insanity. In Babylon, every physician had a personal god, but the top deity was Ninurta, the healing god. The job of the priest was to diagnose the illness and then appeal to the god that specialized in that particular disease.

The ancient Egyptians knew very little about how nerves, muscles or blood vessels worked. Instead, they believed that the parts of the body were a microcosm of what was outside of it. The bones and flesh were the earth, the heart that warmed the body was fire, the breath was wind and the body's fluids were water that ebbed and flowed like the Nile River. The Egyptians did begin to glimpse the truth of at least one mental illness, though. They recognized an emotional disorder that the Greeks later called hysteria. The Egyptians, and later the Greeks, believed that hysteria was not caused by demonic possession but was instead a physical illness. That certainly was a step forward. However, they were a bit confused about which organ was involved, and thought that hysteria—derived from the Greek word for uterus—was caused by a "wandering uterus," resulting from a woman's not being married or not having a proper sex life with her husband.

In general, though, the ancient Greeks thought people who went mad had offended the gods, and in poems and plays told the tales of

Aesculapius healing the sick.

Hygeia, Greek goddess of health.

those so afflicted. For instance, vengeful gods drove Ulysses to plow sand instead of fields. And Ajax, who was bent on murdering his enemies, killed sheep instead after being driven mad by the goddess Athena. To the early Greeks these men were not schizophrenic or manic or depressed, but were driven crazy by the gods.

Greek hospitals at the time were actually temples devoted to the god Aesculapius. Hundreds of these Aesculapian temples were built in ancient Greece and, like today's five-star resorts, were located in the most beautiful and inspirational locales, complete with gardens, baths, meadows and adjacent hillsides. Patients were instructed in personal hygiene and proper diet, but most important was the temple sleep. During this sleep, which may have been drug-induced at times, the patient was supposed to dream of the god Aesculapius, and from him they would be instructed in how to get well. Of course, if dreams didn't come, which often happened, the priests would put on costumes and impersonate

Aesculapius and provide their own view of how health should be achieved. This magical view of healing persisted until the time of the Greek enlightenment when some of history's most influential philosophers and scientists lived. But one vestige of the once-powerful cult of Aesculapius remains to this day. Its symbol was the caduceus, a staff entwined with snakes, which is still the emblem of the medical profession.

Hippocrates' New Direction for Western Medicine

Psychiatry owes a big debt to Hippocrates and his emphasis on the body, and in particular on the brain, as the seat of mental function and suffering. As he wrote: "Men ought to know that from the brain only arrive our pleasures, joys, laughter and jests, as well as our sorrows, pains, griefs and tears . . . I assert that the brain is the interpreter of consciousness."

His knowing that the brain is the home of the mind didn't mean that Hippocrates knew how to actually cure a troubled mind. While he rejected both supernatural possession as an explanation for madness and magic as its cure, advances in chemistry, biochemistry, the invention of the microscope and all the devices of modern biological science would not come for more than 2,000 years. He could not view neurons, nor could he test levels of neurotransmitters in the brain. Instead, he devised a theory of "humors"—life-force elements which, when unbalanced, caused mental disorders and other illnesses. Treatments back then involved certain herbs, blood-letting and laxatives, and were not terribly helpful.

Hippocrates

The Modern View of Mental Illness

A series of crude but effective laboratory experiments in the 1800s clearly demonstrated that the brain was the center of both movement and thought. Some neuroscientists removed portions of the brains of animals to demonstrate that the brain controls movement. In other experiments, in 1864 electrical jolts were applied to the brains of soldiers who received head wounds during the Prussian-Danish War, and doctors found that stimulation on one side of the brain caused the opposite side of the soldiers' bodies to twitch.

Scientists in the late 1800s learned to stain the cells of the brain and observed them under the microscope. By the end of the nineteenth century, scientists knew that the brain was the seat of thought—both deranged and normal— and that it was made up of billions of neurons, all interconnected. But simply knowing these facts did little to advance an understanding of the biology of mental disease, any more than knowing that microbes exist allowed researchers to develop antibiotics. The microscope was invented in 1674, but it wasn't until the mid-1800s that the germ theory of disease began to be accepted, and it wasn't until 1888 that the first antibiotic was developed.

The era of wonder drugs was truly launched when penicillin was released to the public in the early 1940s. But the wonder-drug revolution did not extend to psychiatry until the late 1950s, when the first drugs to treat schizophrenia were developed. In the meantime, a struggle began in the early part of the twentieth century, one that in many ways continues to rage today. This time, though, it wasn't a struggle between scientists and priests. In one camp were those who, like Sigmund Freud, believed that while the mind resided in the brain, personality and behavior were shaped more by external forces and life experiences than by inborn functions of the

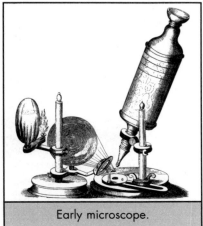
Early microscope.

Blood-letting was once considered therapeutic.

brain. In the other camp were the neuroscientists who felt that the mind was mostly a reflection of what was going on inside the brain at a neurochemical level.

Freud and the psychoanalysts who succeeded him believed that the mind was so immensely complex that it could never be understood through the study of the anatomy and chemistry of the brain. Instead, the key to understanding mental illness was to delve into the mind itself and to explore the dark currents of the subconscious through dream interpretation and long-term psychoanalysis. The psychoanalysts claimed that the subconscious mind rules our waking lives.

Meanwhile, neuroscientists pursued a primarily organic, brain-centered view of mental illness. Cure the brain, cure the mind was their credo. But armed with only a dim understanding of brain biochemistry and structure, they strayed into therapies that today seem barbaric. Neurosurgeons in the first half of the twentieth century subdued patients with electroshock, lobotomies and insulin-induced comas, which only increased public distrust of this organic approach.

Sigmund Freud.

Freud and Psychoanalysis

Sigmund Freud is a monumental historical figure, the "father of psychoanalysis." He was born in what is now the Czech Republic. He attended university in Vienna, then the center of the European intellectual universe. Being Jewish, he found he could only enter certain occupations, namely medicine, industry or business. He chose medicine and gravitated to those studying the brain and physiology, but he found himself drawn to exploring the human mind and the motivations for its actions, and he blended science with philosophy. At the time, treating the mentally ill was considered a difficult and thankless, and thus undesirable, task, which rendered the field of psychiatry especially open to Jews.

Freud's contention was that the unconscious mind plays a major role in the operation of the conscious mind. This notion has certainly been called into question nowadays, but it came to rule the way psychiatrists treated patients for much of this century.

Freud started delving into the subconscious mind at first with hypnotism. Fraulein Anna O. was a 21-year-old woman who became hysterical after her father's death. Her sight and speech were distorted, she was often paralyzed, and was revolted by food. On one occasion, Freud and his mentor Josef Breuer saw that when the woman talked about her problems, the symptoms gradually disappeared. Then when they hypnotized her, they were able to relieve her symptoms to an even greater degree. Freud came to believe that the subconscious mind could influence not just the mind but the body. As he wrote, "hysterical symptoms originate through the energy of the mental processes being withheld from conscious influence and being diverted into bodily innervation." He called this process conversion.

Freud (right) with friend Wilhelm Fliess.

Sigmund Freud, middle, with colleagues in 1911.

Later, Freud discarded hypnosis for a technique he called free association, in which the patient, lying comfortably on a couch, talks freely about whatever comes to mind, no matter how silly or shocking it might seem. Freud believed he could trace the sources of mental conflict as he analyzed this confusing tumble of thoughts, sometimes referred to as stream of consciousness. Freud also felt that dreams could provide powerful insight into the subconscious, but that people dream in symbols instead of directly conjuring up the issue they are wrestling with. So dreams must be interpreted, said Freud. Dreaming of a powerful person, such as a king, symbolizes a parent, and defying that king symbolizes a desire to break with a parent's authority.

Freud was notorious in his time for his belief that many mental abnormalities, such as neuroses, are the result of repressed sexual feelings acting through the subconscious upon the conscious mind. Finally, Freud developed a theory that split the mind into three parts: the id, the ego and the superego. The id is entirely unconscious and is the realm of primitive instincts and desires which seek gratification without thinking of the consequences. The ego rules the conscious mind and tries to strike a balance between the desires of the id and the realities of life in the real world. Then there is the superego which governs the inner acceptance of society's rules and judges between good and evil.

To put these theories into action, Freud and other psychiatrists developed psychoanalysis, which through free association helps the patient become aware of the warring forces inside the mind. But just being aware of inner conflict isn't enough to cure the patient. He found they must vent their frustrations. Consider, for example, a woman who harbors a terrible resentment toward her father. In psychoanalysis, the woman is led to project that hatred onto the therapist, in a process called transference. The therapist, acting as a stand-in parent, doesn't approve or disapprove but simply observes the process. According to the theory, the patient overcomes her hatred and her symptoms subside because she has come to an understanding of and dealt with the original relationship.

Former associates of Sigmund Freud broke away from the grand master of psychiatry and developed their own theories and schools of thought on how the mind should be healed. Chief among the defectors was Alfred Adler, who in 1911 founded the Adlerian school of psychiatric thought. Adler did not hold with Freud's views on the importance of sexual desire in human motivation and mental illness. Instead, he believed people's mental processes are governed more by how they feel they fit in to society. Adler contended that if one develops a feeling of inferiority, through childhood trauma and such, mental illness may result.

Freud first visited the United States in 1909; this visit sparked a revolution in the way Americans view the mind and how it should be healed. Psychiatry in the U.S. came to be dominated by Freud and his disciples and dissenters. The psychoanalytical movement thoroughly dominated American psychiatry from the 1930s to the 1970s.

Freud and his theories mainly dealt with hysteria and other neuroses, a broad category that covers any faulty or inefficient way of handling inner conflict or worry. He did not hold that psychoanalysis would be effective against psychoses, which include such major disorders as bipolar disorder (formerly called manic-depressive disorder) and schizophrenia. In this Freud was right; today most physicians feel that these are primarily diseases of brain chemistry, which usually require lifelong drug therapy.

The psychiatrists who succeeded Freud were not as timid when it came to crossing the line into psychosis. Many of them came to believe that society and its rules were the cause of neurosis and even insanity, and that to varying degrees everyone was a bit crazy. In 1954, the Midtown Manhattan Study came to the startling conclusion that 80 percent of adults had at least some symptoms of mental illness, a claim that today seems absurd. By this standard, practically everyone needed long-term psychoanalysis, and by the 1960s it seemed everyone was seeing a "shrink."

Today's statistics point to about two percent of the population having symptoms of mental illness—such as schizophrenia, manic-depressive syndrome or depression—serious enough to require a doctor's care. Their illnesses appear to be related more to neurochemical malfunctioning of the brain than to repressed hostilities. Psychiatrists currently care for this population primarily with psychopharmaceuticals.

Psychoanalytical theories of how the mind operates in health and mental illness dominated psychiatry until the 1950s, when they began to come under attack. The usefulness of the psychoanalytical approach to curing mental disorders was brought into serious doubt in 1972 when the US/UK Study was published. In this study, 250 British and 450 American psychiatrists were shown identical videotapes of patients being interviewed by psychiatrists. These patients were giving the same information to the same psychiatrist and yet there was massive disagreement among those viewing the tapes as to what was wrong with the patients. Most of the patients who were diagnosed as "depressed" by British psychiatrists were diagnosed as "schizophrenic" by the Americans. These are two dramatically different mental conditions which nowadays are treated quite differently. The study confirmed what critics of psychiatry had been complaining about all along; that diagnosis was unreliable and unscientific. At the same time, advances continued to be made in developing new and ever-more effective psychopharmaceuticals. The fact that these drugs could profoundly alter the course of mental illness proved what many psychiatrists had long been saying—mental illness primarily stems from biochemical dysfunction of the brain. These two camps—the psychoanalytical and the biological—continued to struggle for dominance of the field of psychiatry into the 1980s, with the biological view of mental illness increasingly coming to dominate the practice of psychiatry.

Psychosurgery, Electroshock and Other Desperate Cures

Even as psychoanalysts were exploring talk therapy as the ultimate cure for mental illness, those physicians who were dedicated to the biological theory were developing treatments that in hindsight seem crude—insulin coma and the infamous lobotomy. These were desperate times, though. Medical science was busy vanquishing formerly deadly illnesses with drugs and surgery, and yet the mental institutions of the world were still filled with schizophrenics, depressives and others who had no hope of ever returning to a normal life. Even Abraham Brill, a noted psychoanalyst in the first half of the twentieth century, recognized that drastic measures were called for. As he once wrote: "Schizophrenia is so hopeless that anything 0-that

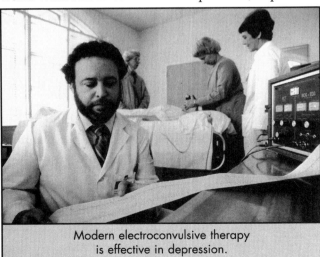

Modern electroconvulsive therapy is effective in depression.

holds out hope should be tried." And just about anything was tried.

Today, the lobotomy is considered a dreadful operation. The prefrontal lobes of the brain are connected to a number of important areas of the brain that deal with thought, emotion and memory. The lobes are far smaller in even our closest primate relative, the chimpanzee, and they are a big part of what makes humans so much more clever than the apes. In severe cases of schizophrenia, they can help produce delusions, hallucinations and phantom voices. A lobotomy cuts many of the connections between these lobes and much of the rest of the brain, particularly the limbic system, which deals with emotion and sensory inputs.

Some surgeons opened the skull and actually removed the prefrontal lobes. Others cut or drilled a hole into the side of the head, inserted a wire or other cutting instrument, and moved it up and down to cut the connections. Walter Freeman invented a method which did

Manfred Sakel peering into an electromicrotome.

not require opening the skull. He first applied a jolt of electricity to the head to stun and anesthetize the patient. He then lifted the eyelids, inserted his cutting devices, and pounded them until they penetrated the orbital sockets, the part of the skull that surrounds the eyes. Then, with a simple left to right motion, he sliced the soft brain tissue.

Without excusing the barbarity of this method, it must be remembered that in the first half of this century, people with severe mental disease usually spent their lives in dreadful institutions. So, lobotomy brought them home. It was considered a wonder cure at the time. What's astounding to consider today is that the Portuguese inventor of the method, Dr. Egas Moniz, actually won the Nobel Prize in Medicine in 1949 for developing the lobotomy. A 1955 stamp issued by Portugal honors Moniz and depicts his lobotomy device.

The problem with the lobotomy is that it transforms a wildly paranoid and sometimes violent schizophrenic into a compliant, docile, but not very bright child. As a result, not everyone was as impressed with lobotomies as was the Nobel prize committee. Nolan Lewis, director of the New York State Psychiatric Institute, said, in the same year that Moniz was being hailed as a medical hero: "Is the quieting of the patient a cure? Perhaps all it accomplishes is to make things more convenient for the people who have to nurse them."

Lobotomized people did indeed need lifelong nursing. In his book *Great and Desperate Cures*, Elliot Valenstein describes the case of "Carolyn," who by 1947 had been institutionalized for 14 years with schizophrenia. She was brought to what is now Yale New Haven Hospital in New Haven, Connecticut, where she underwent a lobotomy of the type developed by Walter Freeman. She later "required" a deeper, more radical lobotomy, and after the operation she was fully subdued. For a certain amount of time she required diapers and was quite confused, as if she had had a massive stroke. But she was calm enough to go home. She was 40 years old at the time of her operation, but for the rest of her life she required a full-time caretaker, as a child would. This was about the best that could be expected of lobotomy.

The worst that could be expected was demonstrated in another case. "J.S." was a man of above-average intelligence from a middle-class family who eventually wound up in Sing Sing Prison for inducing young boys to whip him and have oral sex. While in prison, he consented to a lobotomy to stop his bizarre obsessive behavior, and the operation did seem to wipe away the compulsions for a while. But after his release, he went downhill. He couldn't hold a job for more than a few weeks and was usually fired because he was profoundly unreliable and became quite confused. He eventually wound up in the locked ward of a Veteran's Administration Hospital. He had no control over his bowels; his memory was weak; and worst of all, his masochistic obsession returned.

Another of the desperate cures of the twentieth century was the insulin coma. Insulin is the hormone which controls blood sugar levels. Excessive insulin causes the body to suck too much sugar out of the blood stream, causing drowsiness and even coma. The insulin coma was devised by Manfred Sakel, a physician who worked at a drug treatment clinic. It turned out one of his patients was a famous actress, who was both a drug addict and a diabetic. On one occasion he accidentally gave her an overdose of insulin and she slipped into a mild coma. But when she pulled out of it, her craving for morphine was reduced, and the insulin-coma treatment was born. With insulin, doctors began inducing comas lasting from a week to a month, waking patients up now and then to give them food and take care of other needs. During the procedure, patients were given progressively higher doses of insulin to bring them right to the brink of death, with attendant tossing, moaning, twitching, shouting, and convulsions.

Doctors began applying the coma treatment to other problems, notably schizophrenia, and, according to practitioners, the results were astounding. Sakel held the view that the insulin coma somehow deprived psychotic brain cells of nourishment and allowed normal pathways to reassert themselves. He reported that no fewer than 88 percent of all schizophrenics treated improved. He even treated the famous Russian ballet dancer, Nijinsky, with insulin coma and reported "some success." While some schizophrenics might have improved a bit with the treatment, and some undoubtedly died from the coma, independent studies in the 1930s showed little difference in the outcome of schizophrenics who received insulin coma and those who were left alone.

Electroshock, otherwise known as electroconvulsive therapy (ECT), emerged as another wonder cure for profound mental illness. Apparently, it was first tried out in 1938 by the Italians Ugo Cerletti and

Lucio Bini. Roman police had snared a man wandering about a train station in a state of confusion presumed to be schizophrenia. He was convulsed by an electric shock to the head. It didn't kill him but seemed to wipe out his memory. Later, it was found that electroshock is primarily effective in cases of depression. Cerletti thought it worked by causing the brain to produce vitalizing substances he called acroamines, which were only released during periods of extreme struggle. Whatever the reason, electroshock also came to be widely used to snap people out of deep depressive states. Unlike insulin comas and lobotomies, though, it is still used today in a limited number of cases. It appears to be highly effective when used properly.

Effective Drugs Come on the Scene

The new era in the treatment of the mentally ill was born in 1954 when the Food and Drug Administration approved a new drug, Thorazine. It, and similar drugs that soon followed, delivered such a knockout punch to the lobotomists that very few of these psychosurgical procedures were undertaken by the end of the 1950s. The fact that a drug worked so well in so many serious cases of schizophrenia gave added ammunition to those advocating a biological basis for mental illness. Still more drugs came on the scene, notably lithium, which often had a tremendously powerful effect on patients with bipolar disorder. It decreased the highs of their manic phase and protected them from plunging into the depths of depression.

By the 1960s and even 1970s, the two schools of thought were still divided between environment and nature. Should patients be primarily treated with drugs or with talk therapy? But that tug-of-war came to an end. Today, most neuroscientists and psychiatrists agree that mental illness has a strong biological basis, often requiring treatment with drugs, but that psychotherapy is also effective and can help bring about a cure. This melding of talk and drug therapies, called psychobiology, represents the current wave in psychiatry.

Some psychiatrists fear that the tide has turned too much in favor of the biologists and particularly toward drug therapy. In the 1960s, it seemed that everyone had a "shrink." Today, everyone seems to have a drug, whether it be for schizophrenia, bulimia or just the blues.

Overdosing on
Drugs

T he biological and psychological views of the mind have been at war for most of the twentieth century. The psychoanalysts triumphed in the middle part of the century with their view that mental illness can be explained in terms of an internal battle between ego and id. Today, Freudian psychoanalysis has been largely rejected by most psychiatrists. Long-term psychotherapy, which could stretch over the course of years, is being replaced by relatively brief courses of therapy in which the goal is not so much to "understand" mental disorders as it is to modify behavior and to develop coping mechanisms to deal with the symptoms of mental disorders.

Psychotherapy is in retreat as more mental illnesses are being treated with psychopharmaceuticals—not just psychoses like schizophrenia and bipolar disorder, but also neuroses like obsessive-compulsive disorder and bulimia. And there is some movement toward applying psychopharmaceuticals to mild depression or even so-called character flaws, such as timidity.

This victory on the part of the biological psychiatry camp is not enthusiastically celebrated in all corners of the psychiatric community. There are those who say that we are losing something important. They say we are losing a clear understanding of the roots of personal problems and a deep understanding of psychiatric patients as individuals. The most extreme member of the anti-drug camp is Peter Breggin, a psychiatrist and author who has made a career of criticizing the biological model of mental illness. In his books, *Toxic Psychiatry* and *Talking Back to Prozac*, he is not just criticizing the overuse of psychiatric drugs but the use of any drugs at all. He contends, as other psychiatrists have in the past, that the mind is primarily influenced by its environment, not by its inherent biology.

> Valium was once over-prescribed.

Leon Eisenberg.

He writes: "Dozens of mass-market books misinform the public that a 'broken brain' or 'biochemical imbalance' is responsible for our personal happiness. Yet the only biochemical imbalances that we can identify with certainty in the brains of psychiatric patients are the ones produced by psychiatric treatment itself."

Breggin compares psychopharmaceutical drugs, in particular antipsychotics, to lobotomies. "Surgical lobotomy cuts the nerve connections from the frontal lobes and limbic system; chemical lobotomy interdicts the nerve connections to the same regions. Either way, coming or going, it's a lobotomy."

Among Breggin's critics is Susan Dime-Meenan, executive director of the National Depressive and Manic-Depressive Association. As she wrote in a letter to the editor published in *The New York Times*: "It is astounding that Dr. Breggin dismisses the massive scientific evidence supporting genetic and biochemical bases of depression . . . Indeed, he attacks life-saving treatments for our illnesses, including medications and electroconvulsive therapy. His attack ignores scientifically derived knowledge that has passed the test of rigorous clinical trials and has been endorsed by such prestigious organizations as the National Institutes of Health, the National Academy of Sciences and the American Medical Association."

Breggin makes a valid point—one that is shared by some mainstream psychiatrists. In our rush to save money and time, and in our overenthusiasm for neurochemical explanations and drug therapies, we may be losing something—a rich understanding of the patient as a whole and of how much the mind is influenced by our upbringing and environment. In our zealous embrace of quick mental fixes, we also seem to be losing long-term relationships between therapists and patients that allow the development of rich insights into individual minds. Psychiatric patients are too often seen as a collection of symptoms rather than as individuals with unique personal histories.

As Harvard University psychiatrist Leon Eisenberg puts it: "We may trade the onesidedness of the 'brainless' psychiatry of the past for hat of a 'mindless' psychiatry of the future." No longer do psychiatrists believe that for every mental illness there is a submerged early-life trauma. Rather, they believe that "for every twisted thought there's a twisted molecule," says Eisenberg. This notion that molecules explain everything about the mind has become deeply ingrained in psychiatrists. Nowadays, on meeting a new patient they may gather only a few observations in a 10–15 minute session, make a diagnosis and then prescribe a psychoactive drug. Yale University psychiatrist Morton Reiser noticed this tendency was particularly strong in medical residents. "Most of the residents could and would have learned more about a stranger who was sitting next to them for an hour on an airplane trip than they had learned in these formal psychiatric interviews," he says, lamenting that psychiatrists are throwing away talk therapy in favor of psychopharmaceuticals.

Even as psychiatrists are becoming thoroughly entrenched in the twisted-thought, twisted-molecule concept of mental illness, the public is also jumping on the bandwagon. Chief spokesperson for the biological psychiatry point of view is, of course, psychiatrist Peter Kramer. In his influential book *Listening to Prozac*, Kramer tells of several patients

Psychotherapy is endangered today.

Prozac: Is It for You?

Prozac is the most recognized name in the new class of anti-depressants known as selective serotonin inhibitors. Other new antidepressants go by names like Zoloft, Paxil and Luvox, and they are believed to have fewer side effects than earlier antide-pressants. Currently, these drugs are recommended for such conditions as eating disorders, depression, anxiety, panic attacks, or obsessive-compulsive disorders like chronic hand washing or gambling addiction. Articles and books, such as *Listening to Prozac,* have so captured the public's imagination that now almost anyone who sees themselves as at all unhappy or unfulfilled wants to try antidepressants.

The problem is that these drugs do have side effects. For men taking Prozac, interest in sex may plummet and they may have trouble reaching orgasm. How many men are affected? Drug company literature says two percent, while some studies

who were not simply cured of their depressions but were made to feel "better than well." Kramer found that watching the profound changes that take place in people who respond to Prozac transformed his views on what makes people think and behave the way they do.

In the past, he had viewed personality as something that is slowly acquired over the course of a lifetime. But to his surprise he found that in some patients, "Prozac seemed to give social confidence to the habit-ually timid, to make the sensitive brash, to lend the introvert the social skills of a salesman." In other words, all of these "negative" character traits can be profoundly influenced with a drug, leading him and many others in the mental health community to wonder: what is personality? Many people no longer believe that personality is a unique, personally developed substance laid down through a lifetime of experience. Instead, it is increasingly being viewed as something inborn and genet-

indicate that as many as 34 percent of users may be affected. Another side effect is sleep disturbances and nightmares.

Moreover, antidepressants may not be much better than psychotherapy at producing long-term cures, according to one study. Lewis Baxter studied behavior therapy versus Prozac in treating obsessive-compulsive disorder. Two-thirds of the patients in each group got better. Here is another failing of Prozac; in many cases, the relief ends when the drug-taking stops. Many studies show that patients who receive certain forms of psychotherapy, particularly cognitive therapy, relapse into depression at a much lower rate than those treated with Prozac alone.

Still, for many people who don't respond well to talk therapy, antidepressants are a marvelous aid to getting back on their emotional feet. It can lift them out of the quicksand of depression and return them to a normal level of activity after years of psychotherapy has proven useless. The bottom line: Prozac and its cousins can be powerful but because of side effects, they are not for everyone.

ic, something neurochemical, and something that can be altered with psychopharmaceuticals.

Kramer shows in his book how the boundaries of psychiatry are expanding to include not only the profoundly disturbed but also what might be called the "worried well"—people who are unhappy, afraid, shy or lazy. In the past, the worried well have gotten one of two answers from the psychiatric world: "There's nothing wrong with you, go home," or , "There is something wrong with you; I'm not certain what it is, but we can get to the bottom of it with years of psychoanalysis."

Now the new antidepressants like Prozac and Zoloft, which are more selective than the antidepressants of the past, are offering solutions for the problems of the worried well. Many psychiatrists object to wielding psychoactive drugs like these to tackle relatively trivial problems. After all, is it not through struggle that we gain strength? But psy-

Long-Term Psychotherapy: Squeezed Out by Economics

The goals of psychopharmacology and psychotherapy are pretty much the same—to improve and enhance a person's life. For people with schizophrenia, the goal is to get them functioning and back into society. For those who are depressed, the goal is to make them normally happy and adjusted. The issue becomes one of cost. Most psychiatric drugs cost users or insurers about $60 per month, while a single session of psychotherapy often costs twice that much. For depression, be it major or mild, the patient may have to stay on drugs for years, at a cost of around $700 per year. Meanwhile moderate depression may well yield to a brief course of psychotherapy, say 25 sessions, at a cost of about $3,000 in a year. But the depression may not recur for a couple of years and the patient will stay out of the therapist's office. In just two years' time, even brief psychotherapy is about double the cost of drug treatment. In all fairness, you have to add the cost of some follow-up psychotherapy sessions to the cost of antidepressants, say a total of 10 over two years, and then the bill is about the same.

But compare these two approaches to the long-term psychoanalytical approach, which many psychiatrists still contend is highly effective in a variety of mental illnesses. With weekly sessions stretching over two years, say, the bill hits $12,000 or more. Also, the effectiveness of approach, which requires

chiatrists such as Kramer ask: why not give people who are miserable but who are not diagnosable as "mentally ill" every benefit of modern pharmaceutical science?

After all, Prozac-dispensing psychiatrists do not get their patients

intense involvement of the patient in the process of gaining personal insight, has been difficult to prove. Today, most insurers will only pay for drug therapy and brief psychotherapy with only 25–30 visits per year covered. Often there are lifetime caps put on mental health benefits, as low as $10,000 per subscriber.

Psychologists are dismayed by the market forces that are squeezing the life out of their profession. As psychologist Maureen O'Hara writes: "In California, thousands of therapists, who have helped a generation's worth of people to exorcize their demons and develop the psychological skills necessary to thrive in times of chaos and disruption, are being carved out of the health-care landscape."

O'Hara says that nowadays insurers tell her they "don't believe in psychotherapy," that it is not medically necessary and should be lumped together with personal services like massage and hair dressing. But she argues, just because psychotherapy is expensive—although far less so than bypass surgery, which is fully covered—and insurers do not want to pay for it, does not mean it is ineffective or that subscribers do not need it.

"In these chaotic and overwhelming times, where levels of rage, anxiety and despair are careening dangerously out of control, people may need more than ever the confidential services of caring professionals. We allow at our peril market forces, drug manufacturers and bean counters to establish allowable treatment approaches to mental illness . . . That must remain the role of trained psychological professionals who understand the extremes of human experience because they encounter it every day, firsthand."

the raise, the date, the marriage proposal or more respect. They say they are simply making it easier for the person to do it themselves. And really this is the goal of psychotherapy, too.

Some critics say that there is something almost immoral about pro-

Neuropsychiatrist
Richard Restak.

viding a psychopharmaceutical boost to just about anyone who feels they need one. The drugs prescribed, they say, are like steroids for the mind, giving users an artificial life enhancement, and hence an unfair advantage over those who struggle along without medications. This argument, however, is a bit simplistic, as those who are less competent will usually not advance very far in life whether or not they take medication. The idea, say advocates, is that psychopharmaceuticals will allow people to more easily tap into their inborn talents, to get further faster.

Today's world of cosmetic psychopharmaceuticals is not much different from the psychoanalytically dominated world of the 1950s and 1960s, when studies demonstrated that 80 percent of Americans had symptoms of mental illness. In those days, it seemed everyone was either in therapy, if they could afford it, or in need of therapy. The goal was not just to treat major mental illnesses but to make people more happy, more fulfilled, more loving and more alive. Today, the overanalyzed 60s and 70s might seem a bit silly, but it looks like Kramer has resurrected this view of the mind. Only this time it is the biological psychiatrists and the new antidepressants that will treat the 80 percent of the population who are candidates for some sort of mental and emotional renewal. According to Kramer and others, the future will offer ever-more specific and powerful drugs that will be used to chase away the blues as readily as we now take an aspirin to abolish a headache.

"The availability of increasingly specific medicines should open the possibility of increasing specific modifications to temperament," says

Morton Reiser.

Kramer. "Perhaps the future will bring drugs that can influence narrower functions than 'anxiety and aggression.'"

According to neuropsychiatrist Richard Restak, the most intriguing applications of future mind medicines will be in modifying character and personality. "Ordinarily these are very resistant to change, but drugs are in development that will help stimulate motivation, increase energy levels, and repair feelings of chronic low self-esteem—in short, make many people who are not suffering from a definable emotional illness feel better about themselves and the quality of their lives." When properly and sensibly used, the new psychopharmaceuticals will help people attain the state of being that philosophers and psychologists have long advocated as the best way to deal with a chaotic and uncertain world. Don't try to change the world, change ourselves, suggests Restak.

The view of the mind presented by biological psychiatry is tantalizing because it is so concrete and so simple. With medical imaging we can actually watch the changing patterns of the brain's neural activity as we talk, walk, think, plan and listen. We can also observe dramatic changes in the rates of activity of groups of neurons in different areas of the brain and compare the brain activity of schizophrenics or attention-deficits to normals. And we can watch the activity change when mind medicines are administered

The biological point of view, although it is today's darling, is no more capable of explaining everything there is to know about the mind and the human spirit than was Freud's psychoanalytical theory. Eventually, after the love affair with neurochemistry is over and after scientists have reached the limits of what they can explain with this approach, and when we have not managed to solve all of humanities problems with the tweak of a molecule, then perhaps we can sit back and see what we have truly learned. And what will that be? That remains to be seen as we continue this exploration of the mind.

P H O T O   C R E D I T S

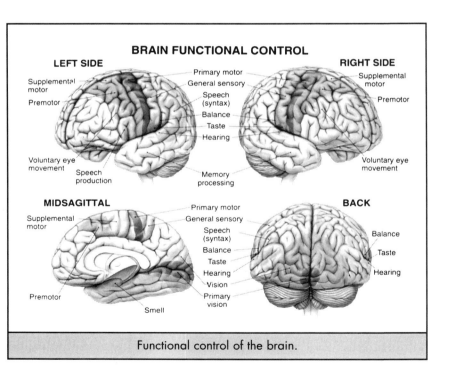

Functional control of the brain.

Nancy Andreasen *The Broken Brain*, Harper & Row, New York, 1984.

Samuel Barondes *Molecules and Mental Illness*, Scientific American Library, New York, 1993.

Richard Bootzin and Joan Ross Acocella *Abnormal Psychology*, 5th edition, McGraw-Hill, New York, 1988.

Peter Breggin, M.D. *Talking Back to Prozac*, St. Martin's Press, New York,1994. *Toxic Psychiatry*, St. Martin's Press, New York, 1991.

Herbert Hendin and Ann Pollinger Haas *Wounds of War: The Psychological Aftermath of Combat in Vietnam*, Basic Books, New York, 1984.

Sudhir Kakar *Shamans, Mystics and Doctors*, Alfred A. Knopf, New York, 1982.

Eric Kandel, et al. *Principles of Neural Science*, 3rd edition, Appleton & Lange, Norwalk, CT, 1991.

Peter Kramer, M.D. *Listening to Prozac*, Viking/Penguin, New York, 1993.

Jerrold Maxmen, M.D. *The New Psychiatry*, William Morrow and Company, New York, 1985.

Vivien Ng *Madness in Late Imperial China*, University of Oklahoma Press, 1990.

Judith Rapoport *The Boy Who Couldn't Stop Washing: The Experience and Treatment of Obsessive-Compulsive Disorder*, Dutton, New York, 1989.

Richard Restak, M.D. *Receptors*, Bantam Books, New York, 1994.

E. Fuller Torrey *Surviving Schizophrenia: A Family Manual*, Harper & Row, New York, 1988.

Elliott Valenstein *Great and Desperate Cures: The Rise and Decline of Psychosurgery and Other Radical Treatments for Mental Illness*, Basic Books, New York, 1986.

U.S. Congress, Office of Technology Assessment *Biological Components of Substance Abuse and Addiction*, OTA-BP-BBS-117, Washington, DC, U.S. Govt. Printing Office, September 1993.

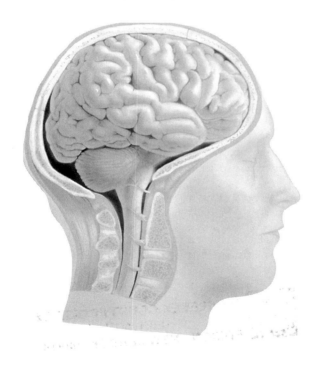

A C K N O W L E D G M E N T S

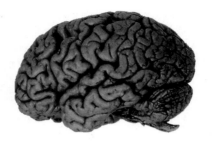

Special Thanks to:

I would like to thank everyone who gave me support and encouragement in producing this succinct book. In particular, I would like to thank my wife Marcie Glickman, Ph.D., a neuroscientist at Cephalon, Inc., and her colleague Kathy Siwicki, Ph.D., a professor at Swarthmore College, for insights into their areas of expertise. Best regards to Luis Gonzalez at Robert Ubell Associates for his perennially cheerful demeanor and encouragement during production of this book. Deep gratitude is owed to Richard Restak, M.D., not simply for writing the foreword but also for thoroughly reading the manuscript and providing detailed and valuable comments. In addition, I appreciate the editorial remarks provided by Robert Ubell and John Rennie, an editor at Scientific American. Lastly, I thank Mike Rivard, M.D., for providing a window into the life of a psychiatrist.

— SCOTT VEGGEBERG

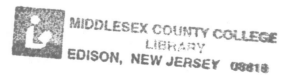